Certified Arborist Exam

SECRETS

Study Guide
Your Key to Exam Success

Dear Future Exam Success Story

First of all, **THANK YOU** for purchasing Mometrix study materials!

Second, congratulations! You are one of the few determined test-takers who are committed to doing whatever it takes to excel on your exam. **You have come to the right place.** We developed these study materials with one goal in mind: to deliver you the information you need in a format that's concise and easy to use.

In addition to optimizing your guide for the content of the test, we've outlined our recommended steps for breaking down the preparation process into small, attainable goals so you can make sure you stay on track.

We've also analyzed the entire test-taking process, identifying the most common pitfalls and showing how you can overcome them and be ready for any curveball the test throws you.

Standardized testing is one of the biggest obstacles on your road to success, which only increases the importance of doing well in the high-pressure, high-stakes environment of test day. Your results on this test could have a significant impact on your future, and this guide provides the information and practical advice to help you achieve your full potential on test day.

Your success is our success

We would love to hear from you! If you would like to share the story of your exam success or if you have any questions or comments in regard to our products, please contact us at **800-673-8175** or **support@mometrix.com**.

Thanks again for your business and we wish you continued success!

Sincerely,
The Mometrix Test Preparation Team

Need more help? Check out our flashcards at:
http://MometrixFlashcards.com/CertifiedArborist

Copyright © 2020 by Mometrix Media LLC. All rights reserved.
Written and edited by the Mometrix Exam Secrets Test Prep Team
Printed in the United States of America

Table of Contents

Introduction 1
Secret Key #1 – Plan Big, Study Small 2
Secret Key #2 – Make Your Studying Count 3
Secret Key #3 – Practice the Right Way 4
Secret Key #4 – Pace Yourself 6
Secret Key #5 – Have a Plan for Guessing 7
Test-Taking Strategies 10
Soil Management 15
    Soil 15
    Water 17
    Mineral Nutrients 18
Tree ID/Selection 20
    Nomenclature 20
Installation and Establishment 24
    Installation 24
Safe Work Practices 28
    Safety Recognition 28
    Work Site Safety Hazards/Appropriate Actions to Be Taken 28
    Rescue Procedure 30
    Climbing/Equipment/Technical 31
    Behavior 32
Tree Biology 33
    Structure 33
    Function 33
    Growth & Development 34
    Biomechanics 36
Pruning 37
    General Principles of Pruning 37
    Techniques 38
    Types of Pruning 39
    Utility Pruning 41
    Recognizing Industry Standards and Best Management Practices 42
Diagnosis/Treatment 43
    Plant Health Care 43
    Diagnosis, Procedures and Techniques 43
    Insect, Nematodes, Diseases and Mites 45
    Diseases 46

ABIOTIC: PHYSIOLOGICAL PROBLEMS, MECHANISMS/STRUCTURE, CLIMATE/MICROCLIMATE, ANIMAL _____ 47
    TREATMENT _____ 48

URBAN FORESTRY _____ 52
    BENEFITS AND COSTS OF TREES _____ 52
    APPRAISAL AND VALUATION _____ 52
    REGULATORY AND LEGAL ISSUES _____ 53
    MANAGEMENT _____ 54
    INFORMATION AND EDUCATION _____ 55

PROTECTION AND PRESERVATION _____ 57
    PROTECTION _____ 57
    DAMAGE _____ 58
    POST-DAMAGE MANAGEMENT _____ 59

TREE RISK MANAGEMENT _____ 61
    RESPONSIBILITY/LIABILITY _____ 61
    SITE ANALYSIS _____ 61
    TREE RISK CHARACTERISTICS _____ 62
    TREE ANALYSIS _____ 64
    RISK BASED ON TREE CHARACTERISTIC FOR LOCATION _____ 65
    RISK MITIGATION _____ 65

TREE SUPPORT AND LIGHTNING PROTECTION _____ 67
    TREE SUPPORT AND CABLING _____ 67
    LIGHTNING PROTECTION _____ 68

ARBORIST PRACTICE TEST _____ 70

ANSWER KEY AND EXPLANATIONS _____ 97

IMAGE CREDITS _____ 125

HOW TO OVERCOME TEST ANXIETY _____ 126
    CAUSES OF TEST ANXIETY _____ 126
    ELEMENTS OF TEST ANXIETY _____ 127
    EFFECTS OF TEST ANXIETY _____ 127
    PHYSICAL STEPS FOR BEATING TEST ANXIETY _____ 128
    MENTAL STEPS FOR BEATING TEST ANXIETY _____ 129
    STUDY STRATEGY _____ 130
    TEST TIPS _____ 132
    IMPORTANT QUALIFICATION _____ 133

THANK YOU _____ 134

ADDITIONAL BONUS MATERIAL _____ 135

Introduction

Thank you for purchasing this resource! You have made the choice to prepare yourself for a test that could have a huge impact on your future, and this guide is designed to help you be fully ready for test day. Obviously, it's important to have a solid understanding of the test material, but you also need to be prepared for the unique environment and stressors of the test, so that you can perform to the best of your abilities.

For this purpose, the first section that appears in this guide is the **Secret Keys**. We've devoted countless hours to meticulously researching what works and what doesn't, and we've boiled down our findings to the five most impactful steps you can take to improve your performance on the test. We start at the beginning with study planning and move through the preparation process, all the way to the testing strategies that will help you get the most out of what you know when you're finally sitting in front of the test.

We recommend that you start preparing for your test as far in advance as possible. However, if you've bought this guide as a last-minute study resource and only have a few days before your test, we recommend that you skip over the first two Secret Keys since they address a long-term study plan.

If you struggle with **test anxiety**, we strongly encourage you to check out our recommendations for how you can overcome it. Test anxiety is a formidable foe, but it can be beaten, and we want to make sure you have the tools you need to defeat it.

Secret Key #1 – Plan Big, Study Small

There's a lot riding on your performance. If you want to ace this test, you're going to need to keep your skills sharp and the material fresh in your mind. You need a plan that lets you review everything you need to know while still fitting in your schedule. We'll break this strategy down into three categories.

Information Organization

Start with the information you already have: the official test outline. From this, you can make a complete list of all the concepts you need to cover before the test. Organize these concepts into groups that can be studied together, and create a list of any related vocabulary you need to learn so you can brush up on any difficult terms. You'll want to keep this vocabulary list handy once you actually start studying since you may need to add to it along the way.

Time Management

Once you have your set of study concepts, decide how to spread them out over the time you have left before the test. Break your study plan into small, clear goals so you have a manageable task for each day and know exactly what you're doing. Then just focus on one small step at a time. When you manage your time this way, you don't need to spend hours at a time studying. Studying a small block of content for a short period each day helps you retain information better and avoid stressing over how much you have left to do. You can relax knowing that you have a plan to cover everything in time. In order for this strategy to be effective though, you have to start studying early and stick to your schedule. Avoid the exhaustion and futility that comes from last-minute cramming!

Study Environment

The environment you study in has a big impact on your learning. Studying in a coffee shop, while probably more enjoyable, is not likely to be as fruitful as studying in a quiet room. It's important to keep distractions to a minimum. You're only planning to study for a short block of time, so make the most of it. Don't pause to check your phone or get up to find a snack. It's also important to **avoid multitasking**. Research has consistently shown that multitasking will make your studying dramatically less effective. Your study area should also be comfortable and well-lit so you don't have the distraction of straining your eyes or sitting on an uncomfortable chair.

The time of day you study is also important. You want to be rested and alert. Don't wait until just before bedtime. Study when you'll be most likely to comprehend and remember. Even better, if you know what time of day your test will be, set that time aside for study. That way your brain will be used to working on that subject at that specific time and you'll have a better chance of recalling information.

Finally, it can be helpful to team up with others who are studying for the same test. Your actual studying should be done in as isolated an environment as possible, but the work of organizing the information and setting up the study plan can be divided up. In between study sessions, you can discuss with your teammates the concepts that you're all studying and quiz each other on the details. Just be sure that your teammates are as serious about the test as you are. If you find that your study time is being replaced with social time, you might need to find a new team.

Secret Key #2 – Make Your Studying Count

You're devoting a lot of time and effort to preparing for this test, so you want to be absolutely certain it will pay off. This means doing more than just reading the content and hoping you can remember it on test day. It's important to make every minute of study count. There are two main areas you can focus on to make your studying count:

Retention

It doesn't matter how much time you study if you can't remember the material. You need to make sure you are retaining the concepts. To check your retention of the information you're learning, try recalling it at later times with minimal prompting. Try carrying around flashcards and glance at one or two from time to time or ask a friend who's also studying for the test to quiz you.

To enhance your retention, look for ways to put the information into practice so that you can apply it rather than simply recalling it. If you're using the information in practical ways, it will be much easier to remember. Similarly, it helps to solidify a concept in your mind if you're not only reading it to yourself but also explaining it to someone else. Ask a friend to let you teach them about a concept you're a little shaky on (or speak aloud to an imaginary audience if necessary). As you try to summarize, define, give examples, and answer your friend's questions, you'll understand the concepts better and they will stay with you longer. Finally, step back for a big picture view and ask yourself how each piece of information fits with the whole subject. When you link the different concepts together and see them working together as a whole, it's easier to remember the individual components.

Finally, practice showing your work on any multi-step problems, even if you're just studying. Writing out each step you take to solve a problem will help solidify the process in your mind, and you'll be more likely to remember it during the test.

Modality

Modality simply refers to the means or method by which you study. Choosing a study modality that fits your own individual learning style is crucial. No two people learn best in exactly the same way, so it's important to know your strengths and use them to your advantage.

For example, if you learn best by visualization, focus on visualizing a concept in your mind and draw an image or a diagram. Try color-coding your notes, illustrating them, or creating symbols that will trigger your mind to recall a learned concept. If you learn best by hearing or discussing information, find a study partner who learns the same way or read aloud to yourself. Think about how to put the information in your own words. Imagine that you are giving a lecture on the topic and record yourself so you can listen to it later.

For any learning style, flashcards can be helpful. Organize the information so you can take advantage of spare moments to review. Underline key words or phrases. Use different colors for different categories. Mnemonic devices (such as creating a short list in which every item starts with the same letter) can also help with retention. Find what works best for you and use it to store the information in your mind most effectively and easily.

Secret Key #3 – Practice the Right Way

Your success on test day depends not only on how many hours you put into preparing, but also on whether you prepared the right way. It's good to check along the way to see if your studying is paying off. One of the most effective ways to do this is by taking practice tests to evaluate your progress. Practice tests are useful because they show exactly where you need to improve. Every time you take a practice test, pay special attention to these three groups of questions:

- The questions you got wrong
- The questions you had to guess on, even if you guessed right
- The questions you found difficult or slow to work through

This will show you exactly what your weak areas are, and where you need to devote more study time. Ask yourself why each of these questions gave you trouble. Was it because you didn't understand the material? Was it because you didn't remember the vocabulary? Do you need more repetitions on this type of question to build speed and confidence? Dig into those questions and figure out how you can strengthen your weak areas as you go back to review the material.

Additionally, many practice tests have a section explaining the answer choices. It can be tempting to read the explanation and think that you now have a good understanding of the concept. However, an explanation likely only covers part of the question's broader context. Even if the explanation makes sense, **go back and investigate** every concept related to the question until you're positive you have a thorough understanding.

As you go along, keep in mind that the practice test is just that: practice. Memorizing these questions and answers will not be very helpful on the actual test because it is unlikely to have any of the same exact questions. If you only know the right answers to the sample questions, you won't be prepared for the real thing. **Study the concepts** until you understand them fully, and then you'll be able to answer any question that shows up on the test.

It's important to wait on the practice tests until you're ready. If you take a test on your first day of study, you may be overwhelmed by the amount of material covered and how much you need to learn. Work up to it gradually.

On test day, you'll need to be prepared for answering questions, managing your time, and using the test-taking strategies you've learned. It's a lot to balance, like a mental marathon that will have a big impact on your future. Like training for a marathon, you'll need to start slowly and work your way up. When test day arrives, you'll be ready.

Start with the strategies you've read in the first two Secret Keys—plan your course and study in the way that works best for you. If you have time, consider using multiple study resources to get different approaches to the same concepts. It can be helpful to see difficult concepts from more than one angle. Then find a good source for practice tests. Many times, the test website will suggest potential study resources or provide sample tests.

Practice Test Strategy

If you're able to find at least three practice tests, we recommend this strategy:

1. Take the first test with no time constraints and with your notes and study guide handy. Take your time and focus on applying the strategies you've learned.
2. Take the second practice test open-book as well, but set a timer and practice pacing yourself to finish in time.
3. Take any other practice tests as if it were test day. Set a timer and put away your study materials. Sit at a table or desk in a quiet room, imagine yourself at the testing center, and answer questions as quickly and accurately as possible.
4. Keep repeating step 3 on a regular basis until you run out of practice tests or it's time for the actual test. Your mind will be ready for the schedule and stress of test day, and you'll be able to focus on recalling the material you've learned.

Secret Key #4 – Pace Yourself

Once you're fully prepared for the material on the test, your biggest challenge on test day will be managing your time. Just knowing that the clock is ticking can make you panic even if you have plenty of time left. Work on pacing yourself so you can build confidence against the time constraints of the exam. Pacing is a difficult skill to master, especially in a high-pressure environment, so **practice is vital**.

Set time expectations for your pace based on how much time is available. For example, if a section has 60 questions and the time limit is 30 minutes, you know you have to average 30 seconds or less per question in order to answer them all. Although 30 seconds is the hard limit, set 25 seconds per question as your goal, so you reserve extra time to spend on harder questions. When you budget extra time for the harder questions, you no longer have any reason to stress when those questions take longer to answer.

Don't let this time expectation distract you from working through the test at a calm, steady pace, but keep it in mind so you don't spend too much time on any one question. Recognize that taking extra time on one question you don't understand may keep you from answering two that you do understand later in the test. If your time limit for a question is up and you're still not sure of the answer, mark it and move on, and come back to it later if the time and the test format allow. If the testing format doesn't allow you to return to earlier questions, just make an educated guess; then put it out of your mind and move on.

On the easier questions, be careful not to rush. It may seem wise to hurry through them so you have more time for the challenging ones, but it's not worth missing one if you know the concept and just didn't take the time to read the question fully. Work efficiently but make sure you understand the question and have looked at all of the answer choices, since more than one may seem right at first.

Even if you're paying attention to the time, you may find yourself a little behind at some point. You should speed up to get back on track, but do so wisely. Don't panic; just take a few seconds less on each question until you're caught up. Don't guess without thinking, but do look through the answer choices and eliminate any you know are wrong. If you can get down to two choices, it is often worthwhile to guess from those. Once you've chosen an answer, move on and don't dwell on any that you skipped or had to hurry through. If a question was taking too long, chances are it was one of the harder ones, so you weren't as likely to get it right anyway.

On the other hand, if you find yourself getting ahead of schedule, it may be beneficial to slow down a little. The more quickly you work, the more likely you are to make a careless mistake that will affect your score. You've budgeted time for each question, so don't be afraid to spend that time. Practice an efficient but careful pace to get the most out of the time you have.

Secret Key #5 – Have a Plan for Guessing

When you're taking the test, you may find yourself stuck on a question. Some of the answer choices seem better than others, but you don't see the one answer choice that is obviously correct. What do you do?

The scenario described above is very common, yet most test takers have not effectively prepared for it. Developing and practicing a plan for guessing may be one of the single most effective uses of your time as you get ready for the exam.

In developing your plan for guessing, there are three questions to address:

- When should you start the guessing process?
- How should you narrow down the choices?
- Which answer should you choose?

When to Start the Guessing Process

Unless your plan for guessing is to select C every time (which, despite its merits, is not what we recommend), you need to leave yourself enough time to apply your answer elimination strategies. Since you have a limited amount of time for each question, that means that if you're going to give yourself the best shot at guessing correctly, you have to decide quickly whether or not you will guess.

Of course, the best-case scenario is that you don't have to guess at all, so first, see if you can answer the question based on your knowledge of the subject and basic reasoning skills. Focus on the key words in the question and try to jog your memory of related topics. Give yourself a chance to bring the knowledge to mind, but once you realize that you don't have (or you can't access) the knowledge you need to answer the question, it's time to start the guessing process.

It's almost always better to start the guessing process too early than too late. It only takes a few seconds to remember something and answer the question from knowledge. Carefully eliminating wrong answer choices takes longer. Plus, going through the process of eliminating answer choices can actually help jog your memory.

Summary: Start the guessing process as soon as you decide that you can't answer the question based on your knowledge.

How to Narrow Down the Choices

The next chapter in this book (**Test-Taking Strategies**) includes a wide range of strategies for how to approach questions and how to look for answer choices to eliminate. You will definitely want to read those carefully, practice them, and figure out which ones work best for you. Here though, we're going to address a mindset rather than a particular strategy.

Your chances of guessing an answer correctly depend on how many options you are choosing from.

How many choices you have	How likely you are to guess correctly
5	20%
4	25%
3	33%
2	50%
1	100%

You can see from this chart just how valuable it is to be able to eliminate incorrect answers and make an educated guess, but there are two things that many test takers do that cause them to miss out on the benefits of guessing:

- Accidentally eliminating the correct answer
- Selecting an answer based on an impression

We'll look at the first one here, and the second one in the next section.

To avoid accidentally eliminating the correct answer, we recommend a thought exercise called **the $5 challenge**. In this challenge, you only eliminate an answer choice from contention if you are willing to bet $5 on it being wrong. Why $5? Five dollars is a small but not insignificant amount of money. It's an amount you could afford to lose but wouldn't want to throw away. And while losing $5 once might not hurt too much, doing it twenty times will set you back $100. In the same way, each small decision you make—eliminating a choice here, guessing on a question there—won't by itself impact your score very much, but when you put them all together, they can make a big difference. By holding each answer choice elimination decision to a higher standard, you can reduce the risk of accidentally eliminating the correct answer.

The $5 challenge can also be applied in a positive sense: If you are willing to bet $5 that an answer choice *is* correct, go ahead and mark it as correct.

Summary: Only eliminate an answer choice if you are willing to bet $5 that it is wrong.

Which Answer to Choose

You're taking the test. You've run into a hard question and decided you'll have to guess. You've eliminated all the answer choices you're willing to bet $5 on. Now you have to pick an answer. Why do we even need to talk about this? Why can't you just pick whichever one you feel like when the time comes?

The answer to these questions is that if you don't come into the test with a plan, you'll rely on your impression to select an answer choice, and if you do that, you risk falling into a trap. The test writers know that everyone who takes their test will be guessing on some of the questions, so they intentionally write wrong answer choices to seem plausible. You still have to pick an answer though, and if the wrong answer choices are designed to look right, how can you ever be sure that you're not falling for their trap? The best solution we've found to this dilemma is to take the decision out of your hands entirely. Here is the process we recommend:

Once you've eliminated any choices that you are confident (willing to bet $5) are wrong, select the first remaining choice as your answer.

Whether you choose to select the first remaining choice, the second, or the last, the important thing is that you use some preselected standard. Using this approach guarantees that you will not be enticed into selecting an answer choice that looks right, because you are not basing your decision on how the answer choices look.

This is not meant to make you question your knowledge. Instead, it is to help you recognize the difference between your knowledge and your impressions. There's a huge difference between thinking an answer is right because of what you know, and thinking an answer is right because it looks or sounds like it should be right.

Summary: To ensure that your selection is appropriately random, make a predetermined selection from among all answer choices you have not eliminated.

Test-Taking Strategies

This section contains a list of test-taking strategies that you may find helpful as you work through the test. By taking what you know and applying logical thought, you can maximize your chances of answering any question correctly!

It is very important to realize that every question is different and every person is different: no single strategy will work on every question, and no single strategy will work for every person. That's why we've included all of them here, so you can try them out and determine which ones work best for different types of questions and which ones work best for you.

Question Strategies

READ CAREFULLY

Read the question and answer choices carefully. Don't miss the question because you misread the terms. You have plenty of time to read each question thoroughly and make sure you understand what is being asked. Yet a happy medium must be attained, so don't waste too much time. You must read carefully, but efficiently.

CONTEXTUAL CLUES

Look for contextual clues. If the question includes a word you are not familiar with, look at the immediate context for some indication of what the word might mean. Contextual clues can often give you all the information you need to decipher the meaning of an unfamiliar word. Even if you can't determine the meaning, you may be able to narrow down the possibilities enough to make a solid guess at the answer to the question.

PREFIXES

If you're having trouble with a word in the question or answer choices, try dissecting it. Take advantage of every clue that the word might include. Prefixes and suffixes can be a huge help. Usually they allow you to determine a basic meaning. Pre- means before, post- means after, pro - is positive, de- is negative. From prefixes and suffixes, you can get an idea of the general meaning of the word and try to put it into context.

HEDGE WORDS

Watch out for critical hedge words, such as *likely, may, can, sometimes, often, almost, mostly, usually, generally, rarely,* and *sometimes*. Question writers insert these hedge phrases to cover every possibility. Often an answer choice will be wrong simply because it leaves no room for exception. Be on guard for answer choices that have definitive words such as *exactly* and *always*.

SWITCHBACK WORDS

Stay alert for *switchbacks*. These are the words and phrases frequently used to alert you to shifts in thought. The most common switchback words are *but, although,* and *however*. Others include *nevertheless, on the other hand, even though, while, in spite of, despite, regardless of*. Switchback words are important to catch because they can change the direction of the question or an answer choice.

Face Value

When in doubt, use common sense. Accept the situation in the problem at face value. Don't read too much into it. These problems will not require you to make wild assumptions. If you have to go beyond creativity and warp time or space in order to have an answer choice fit the question, then you should move on and consider the other answer choices. These are normal problems rooted in reality. The applicable relationship or explanation may not be readily apparent, but it is there for you to figure out. Use your common sense to interpret anything that isn't clear.

Answer Choice Strategies

Answer Selection

The most thorough way to pick an answer choice is to identify and eliminate wrong answers until only one is left, then confirm it is the correct answer. Sometimes an answer choice may immediately seem right, but be careful. The test writers will usually put more than one reasonable answer choice on each question, so take a second to read all of them and make sure that the other choices are not equally obvious. As long as you have time left, it is better to read every answer choice than to pick the first one that looks right without checking the others.

Answer Choice Families

An answer choice family consists of two (in rare cases, three) answer choices that are very similar in construction and cannot all be true at the same time. If you see two answer choices that are direct opposites or parallels, one of them is usually the correct answer. For instance, if one answer choice says that quantity x increases and another either says that quantity x decreases (opposite) or says that quantity y increases (parallel), then those answer choices would fall into the same family. An answer choice that doesn't match the construction of the answer choice family is more likely to be incorrect. Most questions will not have answer choice families, but when they do appear, you should be prepared to recognize them.

Eliminate Answers

Eliminate answer choices as soon as you realize they are wrong, but make sure you consider all possibilities. If you are eliminating answer choices and realize that the last one you are left with is also wrong, don't panic. Start over and consider each choice again. There may be something you missed the first time that you will realize on the second pass.

Avoid Fact Traps

Don't be distracted by an answer choice that is factually true but doesn't answer the question. You are looking for the choice that answers the question. Stay focused on what the question is asking for so you don't accidentally pick an answer that is true but incorrect. Always go back to the question and make sure the answer choice you've selected actually answers the question and is not merely a true statement.

Extreme Statements

In general, you should avoid answers that put forth extreme actions as standard practice or proclaim controversial ideas as established fact. An answer choice that states the "process should be used in certain situations, if..." is much more likely to be correct than one that states the "process should be discontinued completely." The first is a calm rational statement and doesn't even make a definitive, uncompromising stance, using a hedge word *if* to provide wiggle room, whereas the second choice is a radical idea and far more extreme.

Benchmark

As you read through the answer choices and you come across one that seems to answer the question well, mentally select that answer choice. This is not your final answer, but it's the one that will help you evaluate the other answer choices. The one that you selected is your benchmark or standard for judging each of the other answer choices. Every other answer choice must be compared to your benchmark. That choice is correct until proven otherwise by another answer choice beating it. If you find a better answer, then that one becomes your new benchmark. Once you've decided that no other choice answers the question as well as your benchmark, you have your final answer.

Predict the Answer

Before you even start looking at the answer choices, it is often best to try to predict the answer. When you come up with the answer on your own, it is easier to avoid distractions and traps because you will know exactly what to look for. The right answer choice is unlikely to be word-for-word what you came up with, but it should be a close match. Even if you are confident that you have the right answer, you should still take the time to read each option before moving on.

General Strategies

Tough Questions

If you are stumped on a problem or it appears too hard or too difficult, don't waste time. Move on! Remember though, if you can quickly check for obviously incorrect answer choices, your chances of guessing correctly are greatly improved. Before you completely give up, at least try to knock out a couple of possible answers. Eliminate what you can and then guess at the remaining answer choices before moving on.

Check Your Work

Since you will probably not know every term listed and the answer to every question, it is important that you get credit for the ones that you do know. Don't miss any questions through careless mistakes. If at all possible, try to take a second to look back over your answer selection and make sure you've selected the correct answer choice and haven't made a costly careless mistake (such as marking an answer choice that you didn't mean to mark). This quick double check should more than pay for itself in caught mistakes for the time it costs.

Pace Yourself

It's easy to be overwhelmed when you're looking at a page full of questions; your mind is confused and full of random thoughts, and the clock is ticking down faster than you would like. Calm down and maintain the pace that you have set for yourself. Especially as you get down to the last few minutes of the test, don't let the small numbers on the clock make you panic. As long as you are on track by monitoring your pace, you are guaranteed to have time for each question.

Don't Rush

It is very easy to make errors when you are in a hurry. Maintaining a fast pace in answering questions is pointless if it makes you miss questions that you would have gotten right otherwise. Test writers like to include distracting information and wrong answers that seem right. Taking a little extra time to avoid careless mistakes can make all the difference in your test score. Find a pace that allows you to be confident in the answers that you select.

Keep Moving

Panicking will not help you pass the test, so do your best to stay calm and keep moving. Taking deep breaths and going through the answer elimination steps you practiced can help to break through a stress barrier and keep your pace.

Final Notes

The combination of a solid foundation of content knowledge and the confidence that comes from practicing your plan for applying that knowledge is the key to maximizing your performance on test day. As your foundation of content knowledge is built up and strengthened, you'll find that the strategies included in this chapter become more and more effective in helping you quickly sift through the distractions and traps of the test to isolate the correct answer.

Now it's time to move on to the test content chapters of this book, but be sure to keep your goal in mind. As you read, think about how you will be able to apply this information on the test. If you've already seen sample questions for the test and you have an idea of the question format and style, try to come up with questions of your own that you can answer based on what you're reading. This will give you valuable practice applying your knowledge in the same ways you can expect to on test day.

Good luck and good studying!

Soil Management

Soil

SOIL FORMATION AND HORIZONS

Soil profile refers to the distinct visible layers, or horizons, created by the accumulation and separation of various materials in a soil. An assortment of natural processes, including weather, decomposition of living organisms, erosion, and chemical reactions contribute to the creation of distinct **soil layers**. The underlying rock below a soil, also known as **parent material**, is the most significant factor in determining the overall characteristics of a soil. **O horizons** contain organic materials deposited through biological processes on the soil surface. **A horizons** are a mixture of organic and mineral components. **B horizons** are a combination of deposited materials from the O and A horizons. **C horizons** are composed of weathered parent material or bedrock.

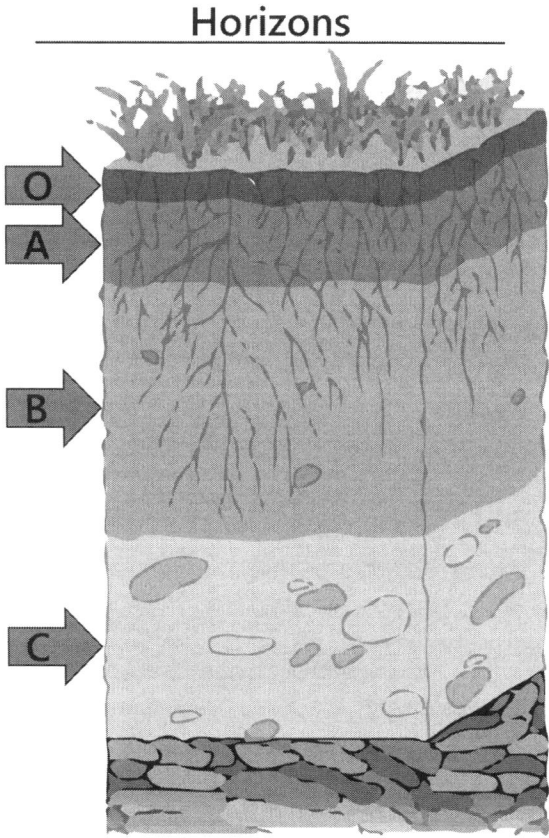

URBAN SOILS

Urban soils can present a challenge to tree growth because they often lack distinguishable structure, are impermeable to water and air infiltration, and can contain pollutants that are toxic to plants. **Urban soil** is also restricted by a lack of **nutrient cycling** caused by the depletion of a healthy O horizon. **Microorganisms** common to native forest soils are also found in lower quantities in urban soils. In fact, the entire **food web** that trees rely on for water and nutrients may be compromised by the limitations of space, temperature, as well as unnatural physical pressures exerted upon trees in the urban environment. The **soil volume** granted to a particular tree may be restricted due to the size and depth of planting holes and can limit potential tree root volume later in life.

PHYSICAL PROPERTIES

Compaction is caused by an array of human actions including paving, pedestrian traffic, grading, and other disruptions to normal soil structure. **Bulk density** increases when soil becomes compacted as a result of collapsing micro- and macropores. Compaction restricts tree root growth by preventing the movement of water and air through the soil, and by the increased friction that growing root tips become exposed to in densely packed soil. Compaction, once it has occurred within a soil, is very difficult to reverse.

LEGUMES

Legumes are plants that, through the development of symbiotic relationships with certain species of bacteria, are able to "fix" **nitrogen** from the environment that would otherwise be unavailable to the plant. The bacteria benefit from chemical compounds released from the plant roots and affix atmospheric nitrogen in knobby growths called **nodules**. Some examples of legumes would include beans; peas; vetches; and even some trees, including locust and acacia trees. When legumes die, they release their fixated nitrogen resources back into the soil in the form of organic nitrogen compounds that are then available to other plants.

BIOLOGICAL PROPERTIES

Fungi growing in and on tree roots will form **mycorrhizal relationships** that are **symbiotic** (benefit both organisms). Mycorrhizal relationships within the roots of plants assist with the acquisition of nutrients and water from the soil while also benefiting the associated fungus by providing it with carbohydrates from the plant. Animals and other organisms reintroduce nitrogen and other nutrients back into the soil as they break down plant materials and form an **O (organic) horizon**. The burrowing of insects and other animals assist in the **aeration** of soil, while bacteria and additional fungi foster complex relationships that **recycle** organic materials as members of a "food web."

CHEMICAL PROPERTIES

Soil with larger proportions of clay, silt, and organic material tend to have a more favorable **CEC (cation exchange capacity) rating**. Sandy soils containing low levels of organic residues will have lower CEC rates and tend to leach nutrients more rapidly. This has to do in part by the **relative surface area** present in the different soil textures. Clay having smaller particles and more surface area allows for more particles to be chemically attached to itself. Sand particles are larger and lack areas of negative charge, making it more difficult to attach to by negatively charged ions such as K+ (potassium).

SOIL IMPROVEMENT

Arborists can improve the texture of soil by incorporating organic materials into the top layers of the soil. **Mulching** can improve movement and retention of water and prevent surface crusting on soil as it dries out. **Air excavation**, with an air-spade or similar device, can add pore space to compacted soil. Chemical problems with soil can sometimes be corrected by flushing with **water** (to remove excess salts) or by the addition of **supplemental nutrients** following a soil test. The pH of soil can be difficult to adjust for a long-term basis, and new plantings should take into consideration the chemical limitations presented by the existing native soil.

STRUCTURAL SOIL

Structural soil is composed of various aggregate materials, including gap-graded gravels, expanded clay or shale, and a hydrogel material to hold it all together. Structural soil is **resistant to compaction** and maintains adequate pore space for tree root growth even when it is loaded under the weight of pavement. Similarly, **suspended sidewalks** utilize plastic or recycled composite cubes that can be lined with special fabric to create a support structure for pavement. The structural cells are filled with an engineered soil that will support the growth of tree roots without many of the problems of sidewalk heaving and ramping common to traditional soil/pavement interfaces.

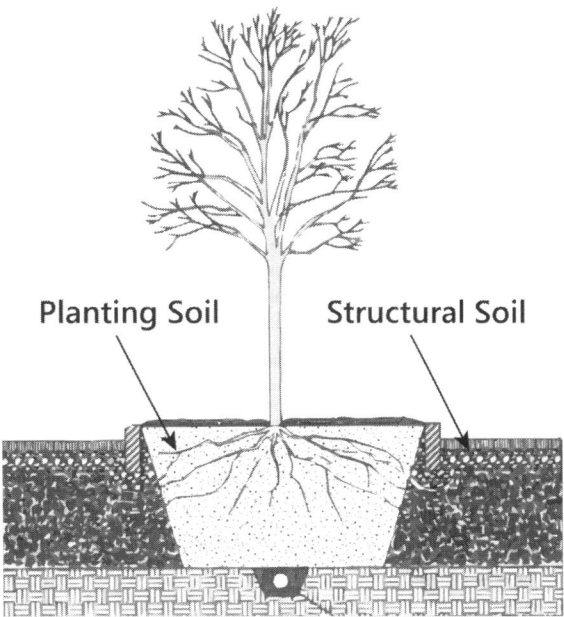

Water

GRAVITATIONAL WATER VS. CAPILLARY WATER

Gravitational water is water that flows freely downwards out of a soil due to the forces of gravity and occupies the **macropore space** of a saturated soil. **Gravitational water** is more prevalent in courser, textured soils such as sand and found to a lesser extent in soils with fine particles such as clay. Capillary and hydroscopic water, conversely, are found in the **micropores** of soil. **Hydroscopic water** adheres strongly to soil, while **capillary water** can move freely through the soil and into roots. Hydroscopic water cannot be absorbed by the plant because it is held too tightly within the soil. A plant can reach its permanent wilting point with hydroscopic water still present in the soil. Capillary water (also known as available water) can move freely through soil and can be utilized by the plant.

PROPERTIES

Plants will adapt their root systems to find underground water sources. An example of this is the **tap root** formed by certain tree species to utilize a subterranean water table. **Annual leaf drop** during dry conditions permits some trees to live in arid locations and the growth of a thick, waxy cuticle on the surface of many tree leaves prevents water loss through transpiration. Plants will also close **stomata** (air exchange openings on the undersides of leaves) to prevent the loss of moisture during dry conditions. Signs of water deficit include wilting and the eventual defoliation of a tree.

Management

Shallow watering encourages tree root systems to grow only in the top layers of soil where water is made available. The uppermost horizons are the first to dry out during drought conditions, and shallow-rooted trees tend to show signs of water stress earlier than deep-rooted trees. Trees that have lost considerable root volume, either through transplant or through pruning of roots, may require supplemental irrigation until they regain a more normal root-to-shoot ratio. **Deep and infrequent watering** will allow the soil surrounding the tree to dry out between irrigation cycles, helps prevent fungal root disorders, and more accurately mimics the conditions of natural rain irrigation.

Water Infiltration

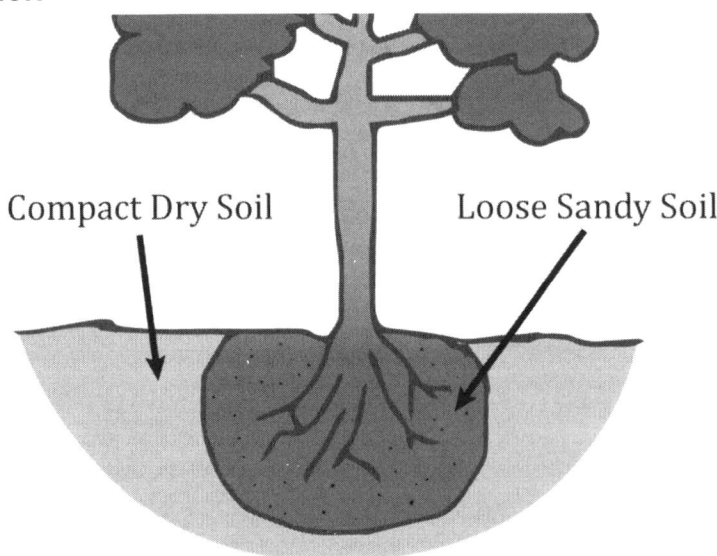

This tree will most likely suffer from **poor aeration** and **limited drainage** from the planting hole into the surrounding soil. The drastically different texture of the two soil types will require the planting hole to be totally saturated before any water can exit, and for the surrounding soil to be totally saturated before any water will infiltrate back into the planting hole. This **interface** between the two soil types will create a "feast-or-famine" water regime known as the teacup effect and is lethal to most trees. To prevent this type of interface layer from being created, it is important for the backfill soil in a planting hole to be similar in composition and texture as the surrounding soil.

Mineral Nutrients

Plant Requirements

Trees suffering from **nitrogen deficiency** will grow slower, have smaller leaves, and take on a yellow appearance due to a condition known as **chlorosis**. Nitrogen-deficient trees will also lack vigor, which can be determined by comparing the **internodal distances** between growing buds on a tree stem. The internodal distances can be measured by comparing the distance between leaves or leaf buds on a growing twig. Fast-growing, healthy trees will have higher internodal distances, while slow-growing trees lacking vigor will have more closely spaced bud placement. Along with nitrogen (N), phosphorus (P) and sulfur (S) are considered **essential macronutrients**. Potassium (K) and calcium (Ca) are considered **secondary macronutrients**.

Fertilizer

N-P-K, or **nitrogen-phosphorus-potassium**, are the three values represented on most fertilizer packages. A fertilizer with the rating 12-3-8 would contain 12% nitrogen, 3% phosphoric acid (P_2O_5), and 8% potassium (K_2O) in the form of soluble potash. An additional consideration for fertilizers used with trees is the **residual salt factor**, the tendency for introduced nutrient compounds to combine and form a salt within the soil. No fertilizer should be used on trees with a salt factor higher than 50. Fertilizers are usually labeled as being slow-release or immediate action. Slow-release formulas are generally preferred for use with trees over fast-acting types.

Soil Analysis and Fertilization

Soil and foliar analysis can give an accurate portrayal of the nutrient content of the soil and a **texture analysis** will yield the relative levels of sand, silt, and clay within a soil. With this information, the arborist can tailor a **fertilizer regime** that will maximize the benefit for the tree while avoiding unnecessary runoff of fertilizers. Cation exchange rate, pH, salt content, and both macro- and micronutrients are generally quantified on soil analysis reports. Unnecessary fertilizer application can sometimes harm trees by encouraging growth of foliage rather than defense systems, exacerbating tree pathogens, and by raising the salt content of the soil. Excess fertilizer is also released into the environment where it can pollute local water bodies.

Buffering Capacity

Buffering capacity refers to the ability of a soil to resist changes to **pH**. Adding an acidic or alkaline amendment to soils with high buffering capacity will have only a reduced or temporary effect. In general, soils composed predominantly of clay and humic (organic) materials tend to have **higher buffering capacity**. Sandy soils and those with lower levels of organic materials will have **lower buffering capacities**. To raise the pH of a soil, **lime** is generally added and mixed into the top layer of the soil to reduce pH ammonium sulfate, or sulfur-coated urea is added.

Tree ID/Selection

Nomenclature

CLASSIFICATION (CONIFEROUS/DECIDUOUS/PALMS)

GENERAL

Coniferous trees include pines, spruces, firs, hemlocks, junipers, and other trees that have evergreen leaves, generally in the form of needles or scales. Conifer literally means "cone bearing" and seeds of conifers are formed in the female cones of a given species. **Deciduous** trees are ones that lose some or all of their leaves during certain times of the year. Deciduous trees are sometimes known as hardwoods, and include oaks, maples, ash, poplars, and other broad-leafed specimens. **Palms** differ from other types of trees in that they grow fronds in lieu of leaves, lack a true xylem—also known as heartwood—and have a single growing bud located at the top of the tree. Because they have only one growing meristem, they generally do not have a branching structure as in conifers and hardwood species.

SPECIFIC

Specific epithets generally follow the **genus name**. For example, *Quercus rubra*, or Northern Red Oak, describes both the genus of oaks (*Quercus*) and the particular species (*rubra*). **Specific epithets** will always be italicized, with the genus name being capitalized and the species name in lower case. It is important to use specific epithets because individual species may have unique growing habits, cultural requirements, disease resistances, and physical appearance. Within a specific species, there may also exist **cultivar names**, which are denoted by single quotation marks with no italicization. For example, *Quercus rubra* "Aurora." For trees that are formed as a hybrid between two different species, the addition of an "x" is included. For example, London Plane tree is written as *Plantanus* x *acerfolia*.

TREE CHARACTERISTICS

GENERAL CHARACTERISTICS

Trees successful in urban environments are able to make use of **limited or highly disturbed soils** and are tolerant to a variety of **stress factors** including pollution, heat, and vandalism. They may also have a **branching structure** that conforms to human activity (such as wide, narrow branch angles that allow trucks to travel beneath). "Design criteria" involves the understanding of the specific function and expectations of a tree within a landscape. For example, a row of densely foliated evergreens planted on the northern side of a property to block heavy winds would demonstrate an understanding of **design criteria** in tree selection and placement.

SPECIFIC CHARACTERISTICS

Desirable tree characteristics include both practical and aesthetic merits found within a given species of tree. These include interesting bark patterns that increase winter appeal, blossoms and fruit that display a variety of colors, and trees that emit favorable odors during bloom. **Undesirable characteristics** would include trees that drop large and messy fruit, have foul odors when in bloom, and create extensive heaving of pavement from roots. Additionally, trees that have extensive histories of pest and pathogen problems, such as American elms (*Ulmus americana*) and their nearly universal susceptibility to Dutch elm disease, would be a disqualifying characteristic for this tree.

Leaf Arrangement

Leaves are generally arranged in one of two ways: **opposite arrangement**, in which leaves are located in pairs directly across the stem from each other at each node, and **alternating arrangement**, in which leaves are singly located on alternating sides of the stem. Two common variations of the opposite arrangement are the **decussate pattern**, in which each pair is rotated 90 degrees around the stem from the previous pair, and the **whorled arrangement**, in which there are three or more leaves at each node. Alternating-leaved species are more common in most parts of the world than opposite-leaved. A way to remember some of the prevalent tree species having opposite leaved stems is by the device "MAD Horse" which refers to maple, ash, dogwood, and horse chestnut.

Compound and Simple Leaves

Simple leaves are those that are made up of a single part, blade, or needle that is attached to a stem by a petiole, or leaf stem. **Compound leaves** will have a number of different leaflets that come together to form the larger leaf structure, oftentimes each with its own petiole. Compound leaves can be categorized by the orientation of their leaflets into pinnate, which is two rows of leaflets along a petiole; bi-pinnate, which has a second order of organization composed of rows of pinnate leaflets; or palmate, in which all leaflets radiate out from a single point on the petiole.

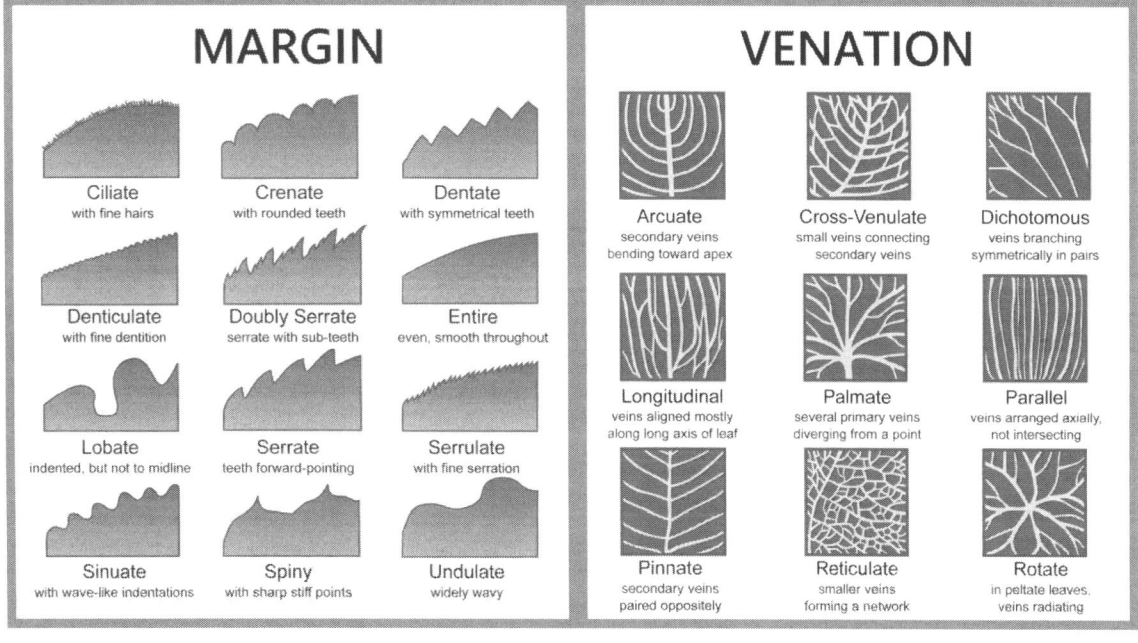

SHAPE & ARRANGEMENT

Acicular
needle shaped

Falcate
hooked or sickle shaped

Orbicular
circular

Rhomboid
diamond-shaped

Acuminate
tapering to a long point

Flabellate
fan shaped

Ovate
egg-shaped, wide at base

Rosette
leaflets in tight circular rings

Alternate
leaflets arranged alternately

Hastate
triangular with basal lobes

Palmate
resembles a hand

Spatulate
spoon-shaped

Aristate
with a spine-like tip

Lanceolate
pointed at both ends

Pedate
palmate, divided lateral lobes

Spear-shaped
pointed, barbed base

Bipinnate
leaflets also pinnate

Linear
parallel margins, elongate

Peltate
stem attached centrally

Subulate
tapering point, awl-shaped

Cordate
heart-shaped, stem in cleft

Lobed
deeply indented margins

Perfoliate
stem seeming to pierce leaf

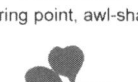
Trifoliate/Ternate
leaflets in threes

Cuneate
wedge shaped, acute base

Obcordate
heart-shaped, stem at point

Odd Pinnate
leaflets in rows, one at tip

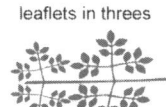
Tripinnate
leaflets also bipinnate

Deltoid
triangular

Obovate
egg-shaped, narrow at base

Even Pinnate
leaflets in rows, two at tip

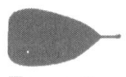
Truncate
squared-off apex

Digitate
with finger-like lobes

Obtuse
bluntly tipped

Pinnatisect
deep, opposite lobing

Unifoliate
having a single leaf

Elliptic
oval-shaped, small or no point

Opposite
leaflets in adjacent pairs

Reniform
kidney-shaped

Whorled
rings of three or more leaflets

Identification

Leaves can be a great way to **distinguish** hardwood trees from each other. The size, shape, leaf base, and margins are aspects of leaves that allow you to quickly narrow down the genus and species of an unknown specimen. Other characteristics, such as the shape and orientation of buds, bark color and texture, and specific smells and tastes are other distinguishing features of trees. **Tree identification keys and guides** can be helpful for new tree enthusiasts and for unusual trees encountered in the landscape or forest. Identification keys give step-by-step instructions based on lists of various visual characteristics that can systematically determine a species.

Selection

Health/Quality/Survivability

Hardiness refers to the ability of a plant to survive the lowest temperatures it is exposed to in a given climatic zone. Plants that are known to be hardy in a specific climate may still perish if they are subject to additional stress factors such as strong prevailing winds, growing in exposed areas, and if they are growing in containers where their reduced soil volume allows for their roots to freeze. Arborists can determine what hardiness zone they are in by consulting a **Hardiness Zone Map**, made available by the USDA. Plants suffering from cold damage will generally decline rapidly due to the death of roots. Conversely, plants growing in warmer climates than they originate from may be more susceptible to various pests and pathogens.

Native Species

Native trees may perform well in their natural range as they are adapted to the local climate and soil. They may also have established resistances to local pests. Oftentimes **municipalities** require some or all new plantings to be **native local varieties**. Disadvantages to using native species include potential difficulty in locating native nursery stock and poor performance of native trees when placed in urban environments. Native trees often do not have the same problem of being invasive reproducers in their native ranges as some introduced species do. **Naturalized species** are those that can grow and reproduce outside of their native soil and have adapted over time to become a permanent fixture within a landscape.

Selecting Nursery Stock

Quality nursery trees will have a well-spaced **branching pattern** with scaffold (or main) branches that are less than half the diameter of the trunk. Branches will also have **open unions** where they split off, creating a "U" shape rather than a tight "V" shape, preventing the formation of problematic included bark later in life. The **base** of the tree will become wider at ground level, indicating a healthy root or trunk flare. The **root system** will be free of circling, girdled, or overly kinked roots. It is important to select trees such as these to maximize the chances of tree survival through early life, and to reduce the maintenance requirements of the tree following establishment. Trees that do not display these signs of good structure and health should be rejected at the nursery.

Installation and Establishment

Installation

SITE EVALUATION

Proper site evaluation takes into consideration the specific **environmental features** of a prospective site, along with the **landscape architect's intent** for how to utilize the site to achieve functional goals. **Site evaluation** should also determine if there are any buried utilities located near the planting site. Limiting factors that may disqualify certain plants for consideration include the hours of daylight available, annual rainfall totals, and the texture and pH of the existing soil resources. Additionally, the mature size of certain trees may restrict their use in certain areas. The crown height, spread, and shape of a grown tree may conflict with buildings and power lines. Certain trees also require greater soil volume than others, and some species are notorious for heaving and cracking sidewalks.

PREPARING PLANTING AREA

The **planting hole** should be at least 2 to 3 times the width and slightly shallower than the depth of the root ball being planted. The hole should be wider near the surface than at the bottom as a majority of the fibrous roots will expand near the surface. When planting in dense clay soils, it may be helpful to dig a hole up to 5 times the width of the root ball. This will encourage root exploration outside of the original root package and aid drainage. Amending the backfill soil is generally not recommended unless the soil is completely incapable of supporting tree health. If this is the case, extensive soil remediation will be necessary prior to planting.

PROPER PLACEMENT OF TREE IN PLANTING AREA

The new tree should be **centered** in the planting hole and at or slightly **above grade**. Soil can be added or removed if necessary, to accomplish this. Ideally, place the tree oriented towards the same **cardinal direction** as it was in the nursery to avoid sunscald on the branches and trunk. Never place gravel or loosely packed soil in the bottom of the planting hole, as this can cause a soil interface that resists drainage and may cause the tree to slump in the hole. If the tree is balled and burlapped, remove at least the top 2/3 of the wire and burlap prior to backfilling the hole. **Backfill** should be lightly tamped to ensure the tree is supported in the hole and to prevent air pockets from forming.

DRAINAGE

Planting too deep is one of the biggest problems facing newly installed trees and can lead to root death and a decline in health. Planting slightly above grade may be helpful in planting sights that have extremely poor **drainage**. In instances like this, the tree can be planted 2-3 inches above grade to allow the upper roots to more easily spread into nearby soil. The backfill soil is then placed around the root ball and tapered up to the root flare, creating a slight mound. Avoiding low areas where water collects and proper grading while preparing the site will help to prevent drainage problems. Another option for improving drainage is the installation of drain tiles or the introduction of organic amendments into the soil prior to planting.

PROPER HANDLING OF PLANTING STOCK

Bare root trees are delicate and must be kept moist until they are planted. They are generally planted during or directly after the dormant season. Oftentimes bare root trees will be sweated or allowed to warm in a climate-controlled area until the buds begin to swell. **Containerized trees**

often suffer from kinked or girdling roots that can cause problems later in life. It may be necessary to pull densely packed roots apart and remove circling roots prior to planting containerized trees. **Balled and burlapped trees** will need to have any artificial burlap or string removed from the root ball and, if they have a wire basket, at least the upper portion of this basket should be removed prior to planting.

IMPACT OF SOIL AMENDMENTS ON TREE ESTABLISHMENT

Rarely is it necessary to combine **amendments** with the backfill soil. The addition of differently textured additives to the planting can cause soil interface problems, as in the **teacup effect**. It was once thought that gravel would assist with drainage, but in reality, it creates the opposite effect by creating an impermeable layer in the soil. If a soil test determines that the soil is lacking key nutrients, it is acceptable to add a small amount of **time release fertilizer** to the soil mix. Small amounts of organic material may not be detrimental to the planting, but large quantities of **organic amendments** may cause the tree to become unstable in the planting hole and the entire plant may sink as organic matter breaks down and leaches from the soil.

PRINCIPLES OF BACK FILLING AND BERMING

Loosely placing backfill around a newly installed plant may cause **air pockets** around the roots that can cause roots to dry out and die as a result. Loose soil around the planting may be more likely to **erode** and trees are more likely to be pushed over during wind with lightly packed soil. Often it is helpful to create a **berm** or dyke around the planting using excess backfill soil to create a basin that will drain into the root package as irrigation is applied. On plantings located on the side of a hill, it is a common practice to build a berm below the planting that includes a channel to allow excess surface water to drain away from the planting following soil saturation near the roots.

POST-PLANTING

APPROPRIATE WATERING SCHEDULE PROGRAM

A **percolation test** can be conducted to determine if water infiltration is an issue at the planting site. A hole 24 inches deep is dug and filled with water. The water is allowed to drain completely into the surrounding soil and then the hole is refilled. If the hole still contains water after 24 hours, it can be determined that the soil has **poor drainage** and root aeration is going to be a problem for most tree species. Careful monitoring during the first season of the planting ensure the soil is being adequately moistened to a depth of 2-3 inches and allowed to drain completely between watering. The use of **irrigation bags** is recommended for trees that will receive less attention, though a schedule for refilling the bags will need to be established to ensure trees receive adequate water.

MULCHING PROGRAM FOR THE PLANTING SITE

Mulching over the roots of trees provides numerous benefits to trees, including reducing the need to irrigate as frequently, improving the consistency of the soil, and providing nutrients to the soil. **Mulch rings** will discourage the growth of weeds and grass, which can compete with the tree's roots as well as giving landscape trees a neat and professional-looking appearance. Mulching too deep, or mulching against the trunk of the tree (mulch volcanoes) can encourage the growth of **fungal infections** leading to crown rot. **Small mammals** will also burrow in deep mulch and chew on bark, causing damage. Large amounts of uncomposted mulch will **deplete nitrogen resources** in the soil as it decomposes.

WRAPPING THE TRUNK

Tree wraps, much like mulch volcanoes, can trap moisture against the stem of the tree, allowing for the growth of fungal pathogens. Tree wraps can also provide a place for insects that feed and live in bark tissue to hide and reproduce. They can potentially cause extreme temperature fluctuations that may damage tree tissues. Occasionally, **plastic tubes** are placed around the trunks of small trees to prevent damage from beavers and other mammals and to allow for weed eating around the stem. If anything is to be placed around the tree that will not disintegrate in the environment, there should be a plan in place to remove the wrap before it can cause damage to the growing trunk.

Tree Support and Protection System

Small trees are generally supported with two or three **stakes**, with at least one located on the windward side and driven into the soil outside of the root package. **Webbing** or other soft flexible textile material is strung between the trunk and the stake as low as possible while still providing support. The wire-and-hose method is no longer recommended for guying trees, as it can cause **girdling** to the tree if it is not removed early on in the tree's life. Guys and stakes should be checked at least twice during the first season of the new tree's life. Leaving the system on longer than necessary can cause poor trunk taper and lead to a poorly developed root system.

Pruning

While it is not recommended that trees be structurally **pruned** at the time of planting, it is acceptable to remove any branches that were damaged during transport. Pruning within the first years following establishment can prevent structural problems that will require greater attention later in life. The **leader** of a tree is the most central and upright stem on a tree. A **codominant stem** will have a diameter nearly as thick as the central leader and is usually connected to the main leader at a narrow V-shaped union. Codominant stems are considered a **structural weakness** for the tree and early detection and subordination can prevent tree failures later on in life.

Planting Time

Bare-root trees do not have extensive, established root systems like containerized plants and are more vulnerable to stressing factors such as extreme heat or dry conditions. For this reason, it is important to plant bare-root trees during the **late winter or early spring**. It is critically important to not plant bare-root stock at the time of **bud break**, as the tree is in a physiologically vulnerable state when experiencing its "spring flush" of new flowers or leaves. Bare-root stock is generally small in size, but historically, larger trees were transplanted bare root with great success, especially if they are held in cold storage prior to planting. Large caliper bare-root stock is making a comeback due to the invention of **hydrogels** that can be sprayed on the root systems of bare root-trees, preventing desiccation of roots during storage and transport.

Fertilizing and Early Establishment

Excessive fertilization of young trees can cause damage to young roots in a condition known as "**fertilizer burn**." Additionally, large amounts of **nitrates** can cause excessive leaf growth that can stress a root system that may not be developed enough to support a rapidly growing canopy. Adding small amounts of slow release fertilizer with a low salt factor can sometimes safely increase growth and establishment of trees, though effects will not be noticed until at least the second year after planting. **Mulching** will generally provide a greater benefit to the tree than any fertilizer application can.

Transplanting

Principle

Transplanting during the **dormant season** is generally recommended for trees that are notoriously difficult to transplant. Digging the largest **root ball** possible to retain the greatest quantity of roots will also maximize the chances of success. Proper **root pruning** prior to transplanting can help form a dense root ball reminiscent of a containerized plant, which is also recommended with some species. During transport, **antitranspirants** applied to the foliage may help with water loss, and irrigation following transplant will be important while the tree is establishing. For larger trees, **in-tree misting irrigation** may be recommended to further mitigate effects of transplant shock.

TECHNIQUES

Root pruning, like branch pruning, results in vigorous growth below the cut and can help to consolidate a meandering root system into a denser and more easily transplantable package. A clean, sharp **spade** is pushed down consecutively around the root ball in a circular pattern. Sometimes root pruning is conducted several years in a row, each time in a concentric pattern a few inches past the previous pruning. When the tree is finally transplanted, there should be a dense mat of new roots forming near the outside of the root ball. Larger trees being transplanted with an excavator may be root pruned by hand with **loppers** and **saws** to clean up rough cuts created by the machine.

TRANSPLANT SHOCK

Transplant shock is a physiological response trees have to stresses brought upon them through the transplant process and are generally due to the loss of roots leading to a **water deficit** within the tree. **Broadleaf plants** benefit from transplant during dormant seasons because they are not transpiring water through leaf stoma during the winter and early spring. The loss of roots prevents the tree from accessing water resources in the soil until new roots have established. **Young trees** tend to deal with transplant shock better than older trees and will have a shorter recovery period. Proper **irrigation** following transplant is the best way to help lessen the effects of transplant shock.

TRANSPLANTING COLLECTED STOCK WILDLINGS

Volunteer stock sourced from **forested areas** tend to have long meandering roots that are difficult to maintain when transplanting. Trees growing wild in a **woodland environment** may also be genetically predisposed to living in deep, rich forest soils and adapt poorly to drier, more compacted sites. Trees growing in **open areas** tend to have denser root systems, greater branch structure, and are more likely to adapt to a new environment than forest seedlings. Wildlings are best transplanted during the **dormant season** or after they have hardened off in late spring. Wild stock may have the added advantage of roots that are already inoculated by beneficial **mycorrhizal fungus**, some of which are required by root systems of native trees.

Safe Work Practices

Safety Recognition

RECOGNIZING INDUSTRY STANDARDS

The term "**should**" denotes a practice or behavior that is recommended by safety standards but is not necessarily required by law. The term "**shall**," when found in safety literature, refers to actions that, if not followed, could result in punitive action from OSHA or other regulatory bodies governing tree work. If an arborist is unsure about a piece of gear, or allowable application of a piece of equipment, they may consult **ANSI Z133** or **29 CFR** of OSHA's General Industry Standards. Arborists should also be aware of certain **local ordinances and regulations** that may govern how they conduct arboricultural practices.

Work Site Safety Hazards/Appropriate Actions to Be Taken

PERSONAL PROTECTION EQUIPMENT

A ground worker making chainsaw cuts at ground level would have to be wearing a minimum of protective eye-wear, approved hearing protection, work boots, a helmet, and chainsaw protected chaps or pants. Gloves are also highly recommended but not required by ANSI standards. The ground worker's chainsaw should also be in good working order, sharp, and with all safety features fully operational. A **medical kit** including trauma dressings should be easily accessible to the entire crew. Equipment for **aerial rescue** should also be present if climbing or aerial lift operations are being conducted.

HAZARD RECOGNITION

According to ANSI Z133, an **electrical conductor** is any overhead or underground electrical device capable of carrying electric current, including communications wires and cables, powerlines, and other such fixtures or apparatus. This also includes anything that may be in contact with an electrical conductor, such as a fence, tree, or vehicle that has contacted a live service line. **Direct contact** occurs when a person or piece of equipment makes contact with an energized conductor, while **indirect contact** refers to the creation of electrical flow through an intermediate object such as a branch or even the ground in some cases.

TRAFFIC CONTROL

When tree crews are working along roadsides, the possibility of a tree or tree part contacting a person or vehicle is very likely without conspicuous **signage and barriers** to warn other individuals traveling nearby. Also, tree workers are struck and killed by motor vehicles every year because there was a poor or absent **traffic control plan** for the worksite. Local regulations generally will outline how traffic control operations will be conducted and what signs, cones, and types of highly visible **barriers** are required in a jurisdiction. Brightly colored **uniforms or vests** are generally required for working near roadsides as well.

PLANNING/ORGANIZATION/JOB BRIEFING

A good job briefing will explain the scope of work being completed and outline specific tasks designated to various workers. Any **hazards** that may be created by the work location, conditions of the tree, and any potential targets (items, structures, or activities) that may be interrupted or damaged by tree care operations should be identified during the job briefing. Whether there is any special **safety equipment** necessary or any areas that will be assumed as "drop zones" should also be identified during this briefing. It is also required that a person trained in **aerial rescue and CPR** (cardiopulmonary resuscitation) be present on a jobsite where climbing is being conducted.

Communication

The command and response system ensures **clear communication of hazards** from climber or ground worker. When a worker is in a tree, they will call "stand clear" before making any cuts with a chainsaw or handsaw. Each ground worker will respond with "clear" when they are out of harm's way, with the final crew worker calling out "all clear." Only after the climber has heard "all clear" will they cut the branch from the tree and allow it to fall to the ground. In addition to verbal communication, tree workers may also utilize **hand signals** if they have a pre-established plan for this, or by **radio communication**. No climber should ever work aloft without another worker within voice range, and a plan should always be in place to alert emergency services if there is an accident.

Chainsaw Kickback

Chainsaw kickback is a dangerous problem that is generally preventable through the proper use and maintenance of chainsaws. When the upper quadrant, located directly above the bar sprocket, comes in contact with an object during operation, the chainsaw may violently **kick back** towards the operator. The **chainsaw break** is meant to help injury from this phenomenon and should always be in proper working order but preventing kickback by using **proper body positioning** should always be practiced. Special concern should be paid to preventing kickback when climbing and cutting using a chainsaw. The user's head and other body parts should never be positioned in a way where they can come in contact with a chainsaw kicking back.

Fuel and Fuel Storage

Fuel should be stored in correctly labeled containers that meet any requirements put forth by OSHA as well as state and local laws governing transportation of **volatile fuels**. Trucks, chippers, chainsaws, and other equipment should always be turned off while being refueled and smoking is strictly prohibited around fueling sites. No gas or diesel equipment is to be started within 10 feet of fueling areas to prevent ignition of spilled fuels. All vehicles are to be equipped with **fire extinguishers** and employees should be trained in their proper use. A **spill kit** should also be available for crew members to clean up any fuel or other toxic substances and prevent their release into the environment.

Training/Safety Skills

When working with a **brush chipper**, it is required that arborists wear all **PPE**, including helmet, eye protection, and hearing protection. It is essential that workers not have any loose clothing or equipment on their bodies that could become snagged and pulled into the chipper. Brush should be fed into the chipper from the side of the hopper and in a manner where workers can easily move to the side of the chipper and avoid being hit by swinging branches. When **maintenance** is being conducted on brush chippers, it should be ensured that the key has been removed from the ignition, that the chipper disk or drum has completely stopped moving, and that the lock pin has been inserted. The wheels of chippers will always be chalked when being worked on.

Felling Techniques

The use of a **tagline** or **pull line** placed in a tree to be felled can help ensure that the tree goes in the correct direction. The feller should ensure that their notch has been properly placed and that all other workers not directly assisting with the felling are at least two tree heights away. All trees with a diameter over 5 inches should have a tagline installed and arborists can use felling wedges to help control the direction the tree is felled. Before any tree is felled, there should be a plan for a **retreat path** for both the feller and the person pulling the rope. Escape should be made 45° to the direction of fell in either direction.

Notch Types

The **conventional notch** is even with the ground on its bottom side and angled upwards at roughly 45° on its upper side. Conventional notches will generally close before the tree strikes the ground, guaranteeing that the tree separates at the hinge. **Humboldt notches** are the same as conventional notches, but oriented with the flat side on top. These are used on extremely large trees where notched wood can be so heavy that it is difficult to remove from the cut. **Open-faced notches** are generally recommended for normal felling operations as they allow the notch to guide the tree for the greatest amount of time before breaking. The back cut should be made directly towards the corner created by the notch, if not slightly above, to prevent the tree from jumping back towards the feller.

Barber Chairs

Barber chairs occur when a tree splits vertically down the trunk as a result of excessive shear force created by the falling tree. Trees with internal decay or with heavy leans may be more susceptible to **barber chairing**. Specialized techniques such as **plunging cuts** and **strapping the trunk** to prevent splitting are methods used on trees where barber chairs are likely. The area directly behind the tree is the most dangerous place to be if a barber chair occurs, so it is important that no crew member be in this area as the tree is felled.

Chipper Safety

Arborists using brush chippers should ensure that they are wearing all **PPE** including eye protection, ear protection, helmet, and work boots. Operators should be free of any loose clothing or jewelry and should not be wearing a climbing harness or anything that could be snagged and pulled into the chipper. No body part should ever enter the **chipper hopper area** and material should be fed into the chipper from the sides. When chipper maintenance is being conducted, the proper **lock out tag out procedures** should be observed, and the **key** should be removed from the ignition and kept in the pocket of the person working on the chipper.

Aerial Lift Procedures

Aerial lifts should be **inspected** daily before leaving the work yard to ensure that all components are working correctly. Workers are injured annually due to both malfunctions and improper use of aerial lifts. Operators should have training on the safe usage of equipment before use and documentation is required by OSHA of **regular training sessions**. When working from the basket, operators should be aware of all nearby objects and hazards, including traffic and electrical conductors. Workers should always be oriented towards the direction of travel to ensure that they are observing minimum approach distances to **electrical conductors**. Regular **rescue training and bail-out procedures** must also be routinely practiced by operators and documented by employers.

Rescue Procedure

Techniques of Aerial/Bucket Rescue

After ground workers have determined that there is an emergency, they will call 9-1-1 and stay on the line with the dispatcher until they arrive on scene. They will report any pertinent details of the accident, including the nature of the injury, the location of the worksite, and if it is a **high angle**

rescue that is required. The worker will then survey the scene and determine if there is any **electrical risk** or any other hazards that would make rescue impossible. The rescuer will try and make verbal contact with the victim and begin assessing the victim to determine the extent of the injury and to see if a **self-rescue** is possible. If it is determined that an **aerial rescue** is necessary, the rescuer will ascend the tree in the safest manner possible and render aid to the wounded person.

First Aid

A person will require **CPR** if they are non-responsive, non-breathing, and have no discernible pulse or heartbeat. 9-1-1 should be contacted upon discovery of an individual with no pulse and CPR should be commenced by certified personnel onsite. The injured person will be placed on a solid surface with their back to the ground. An airway will be established by the head-tilt method or modified jaw thrust and it will be determined if there is a pulse or breathing. If not, two rescue breaths will be delivered, followed by 30 well-placed chest compressions. This will pattern will be continued until the arrival of **definitive care** (EMS) or an **AED machine** arrives on-scene.

Climbing/Equipment/Technical

Types, Use, Maintenance, and Inspection of Climbing and Safety Equipment

A **pre-climb inspection** of gear should include all stitching and componentry of the **climbing saddle**, especially the bridging material and critical load-bearing parts. Carabiners, snaps, ascenders, lanyards, and ropes should all be inspected for excessive wear or damage. Helmets, boots, eye protection and other **PPE elements** should also be closely inspected for wear, and repair or replacement should be conducted prior to climbing. **Rope** that displays broken strands, malformation, glazing, or seems non-uniform in shape or flexibility should be retired from use. Rope that has exceeded its rated cycles to failure or has been exposed to chemical contaminants should also be removed from service.

Techniques When Climbing/Working in and Around Trees

In **moving rope (or double rope) technique (DRT)**, it is common to ascend a rope by means of footlock or hip thrusting. Double rope involves using a bight of rope traveling over a tie in point and back to the climber, where they may adjust the length of doubled rope in the system. Working on a doubled rope puts half of a climber's weight on the tie in point and allows for easy adjustment of slack while climbing. **SRT, or single rope technique**, allows for easier ascent of trees, and movement about the canopy is not restrained by a fair lead to the tie in. SRT is also preferred by many for spar work where a climber may have a cinching attachment point to the tree for fall protection.

Techniques and Equipment Used in Rigging and Tree Removal

To ensure the safety of nearby targets in a **built-up environment**, such as pruning conducted on a tree that overhangs a house, **rigging** is generally employed to ensure the safe, controlled lowering of tree material. A **landing zone** will be established amongst the crew prior to rigging operations. An **arborist's block** will be attached, by way of a rope sling, to a strong upright branch or union in the tree, equipped with a **rated load line**. The load line can be tied to branches using appropriate knots (clove hitch, running bowline) and loaded into a **friction device**, such as a porta-wrap, by the ground worker. The arborist will consider load-bearing characteristics for each component in the rigging system, as well as bend ratios and other geometric aspects of the rigging arrangement.

DIFFERENT TYPES OF ROPE

3-strand rope is relatively stretchy, and weaker than some other types of rope. It was commonly used as climbing lines and/or load lines and works well for natural crotch rigging. **16-strand rope** replaced 3-strand as most arborists' climbing line and is composed of 16 outer strands that bear much of the load, though it does have an internal core. **Double braid**, or **24-strand rope**, has come to be the dominant rope for most modern arborists for climbing and rigging and includes a braided cover and core that share the load. Double braid is lightweight, strong, and is not overly elastic. **Cycles to failure** refers to the number of times a rope can be put under a specific load before it breaks. The **tensile strength** refers to the tested breaking strength of an unused rope.

KNOTS

Knots are a combination of bights and loops organized to perform specific functions. **Termination knots** allow ropes to be attached to carabiners and anchor points. **Bends** allow two ropes to be tied together; **stopper knots** prevent climbers from repelling off climbing lines; and **hitches** perform a variety of functions, including terminations, to an anchor or another rope. **Climbing hitches** are a specific type of knot that allows climbers to ascend or descend a climbing line. It is important that all knots are tied, dressed, and set to ensure that they do not come undone while climbing or rigging.

Behavior

CUTTING ALOFT

The simplest cut available to arborists is the **drop cut**. The drop cut allows arborists to safely and efficiently cut large or small limbs from a tree and cause them to fall straight downwards towards the ground, or into the rigging. **Snap cuts** are useful when arborists want to be able to handle smaller pieces and throw them to a pre-determined landing zone below. The **hinge cut** is used when a longer branch or piece of trunk wood needs to be directed away from a target, or when used in tandem with rigging to ensure the branch smoothly engages the rigging and swings away from the climber. It is crucial to create a plan prior to cutting and to ensure all personnel and equipment on the ground are in a safe location.

Tree Biology

Structure

GYMNOSPERMS, ANGIOSPERMS

Angiosperms are plants that grow an **ovary**, or seed-bearing organ, such as the fruit of an apple to protect and assist with the dispersion of their seeds. **Angiosperms** often have conspicuous flowering parts and are further divided into monocots and dicots based on the number of seed leaves (cotyledons) that arise from germinating seeds. *Monocots* will always have one seed leaf, and *dicots* will have two. **Gymnosperms** generally do not have conspicuous flowers and produce a "naked seed" in a **cone**. Gymnosperms include all pines, fir, spruce, cypress and even the ancient broadleaved gingko tree.

PALMS

Palms are monocots that typically only grow in tropic and sub-tropic areas of the world. They have broad, sectioned leaves that are known as **fronds**, arising from a single bud located at the top of the tree. The trunk of the palm does not contain a true xylem or heartwood, but a bundle of vascular tissues that more resembles a grass stem. As angiosperms, palms produce flowers and fruit, which can sometimes become quite large as in the date palm or coconut palm. Special techniques to prune palms are required, and **ANSI A300 *Pruning Standards*** outlines specific details for palm pruning.

Function

PHOTOSYNTHESIS

Photosynthesis takes place in specific organelles called **chloroplasts** found within leaf cells on plants. These contain the compound **chlorophyll** and, through a series of chemical reactions, combine water, carbon dioxide, and sunlight to create carbohydrates. Chlorophyll is the compound responsible for the green color of most plant leaves and stems. **Oxygen** (O_2) is a byproduct of photosynthesis and is released out of the stomata located on the underside of leaves. **Photosynthate**, or the product of photosynthesis, is stored by the plant for use in cell respiration, a process facilitating the growth and maintenance of plant cells. Photosynthate can be thought of as chemical energy that is ready to be released where and when the plant needs it.

RESPIRATION

Respiration is the process by which trees use stored carbohydrates to release chemical energy that can build and repair cells, thus maintaining life within the tree. **Glucose** (sugar) is the product of photosynthesis that is utilized, along with **oxygen**, to conduct cellular respiration in plants. If a plant is not able to produce enough glucose to replenish what is used through respiration, the plant will eventually die. Leaves introduce oxygen through their **stomata** while stems use formations known as **lenticels** to pull O_2 into living tissues below the bark. Roots acquire oxygen through the **root hairs** to conduct respiration within the root system and this is why it is crucial for soil to contain a quantity of open porous space not occupied by solids or water.

XYLEM AND WATER TRANSPORT

Water travels from the roots of a tree up the stem and to the leaves by way of the **xylem tissues** (sapwood and heartwood). The release of water through the leaves, known as **transpiration**, causes a pressure differential between the top of the tree and the roots that causes water to rise against the pull of gravity. Like liquid traveling up a straw, this "transpiration pull" allows trees to regulate the hydration of the stems and leaves. When an inadequate amount of water is supplied, as in the case of drought, the plant's leaves will lose **turgidity**, causing them to wilt. **Stomata** in the leaves will close and prevent the loss of water, helping to preserve the plant at the cost of diminished photosynthesis.

PHLOEM

The tree phloem is responsible for the transport of **sugars**, created in the leaves, to other parts of the plant. Gymnosperms contain **sieve cells**, while angiosperms use a combination of cells including sieve tube elements and companion cells that actively transport nutrients through the tree, consuming energy. Phloem is formed on the outer side of the **cambium**, and along with the xylem, comprise the flexible fibrous stems and trunks of trees. A majority of the simple sugars (glucose, sucrose) are sent through the phloem to the roots to assist with growth and storage while some is maintained by the above-ground parts of the tree to assist with the maintenance and development of the leaves and branches.

STORAGE

Trees store a great deal of excess carbohydrates in their roots and, to a lesser extent, in stems. **Complex nutrients**, like oils and fats, are often devoted to seeds and fruit to assist with procreation. **Mineral nutrients** are stored within the living and non-living xylem cells of tree stems along with water. **Proteins** are found throughout the tree, but in a highest concentration in seeds, which is why plant seeds are often eaten by animals. A **sink** refers to a part of a plant that consumes energy resources, rather than creating them. An example of a sink would be the flowers and seeds of a mature red maple tree.

PLANT HORMONES

Plant hormones play a variety of functions within a tree, including the regulation of cell elongation and division. They also aid in leaf senescence (leaf drop) and the production of roots, buds, and flowers. **Auxin** is the hormone that causes shoot elongation and is what enables phototropism (growth towards light). Auxin is found in greatest concentrations near the growing tips of plant stems and works in tandem with the root hormone **cytokinin** to maintain root-to-shoot ratio. Artificial sources of auxin are also available and are used by the nursery industry to assist with propagation of plants from cutting.

EXCURRENT AND DECURRENT FORMS

Tree species that have strong apical control and a single, clearly defined, and central leader are said to display **excurrent** growth. Pines, spruce, and other conifers tend to grow excurrently while hardwood trees such as oaks and maples tend to have more **decurrent** growing habits. Trees that grow in dense forests tend to have a more excurrent structure than those growing in an open area.

Growth & Development

SEXUAL REPRODUCTION

Monoecious trees have both the male and female flowers displayed on the same plant, while **dioecious** trees will have a completely male or completely female version of the same plant. Hollies (Ilex) and gingko (Gingko biloba) trees are examples of dioecious trees, while pines (Pinus) and oaks (Quercus) are examples of monoecious trees. It is important to remember that, even though monoecious trees have both flower types, they may not be able to **self-pollinate**, as in pecan (Carya illinoinensis), and may require two separate specimens present to produce seeds.

MERISTEMS

Meristems are the tissues of plants capable of cell division and can be found at the tips of shoots, roots, and within the vascular cambium of the tree. **Apical buds** are responsible for primary growth of trees and allow the tree to grow taller as cells divide. Secondary growth occurs in the **cambium** and leads to increased girth in the trunk, branches, and large roots to aid in the support of the growing tree. Meristematic cells are capable of **differentiation** or can grow into a variety of different types of cells from a single undifferentiated "mother cell" in the cambium. This is how the cambium can produce both xylem and phloem from the same set of cells.

CROSS SECTION OF THE TREE

The **outer bark**, consisting of the cuticle, epidermis, cork cells, and cork cambium, is found outside of the phelloderm and cortex of the inner bark. Within the **cortex**, the phloem is found, followed by the vascular cambium and xylem. The **xylem** can be subdivided into sapwood, which is the living outer section, and heartwood, which is composed of dead wood cells. Palm trees have vascular bundles interspersed within the trunk, lack a true bark, and are not capable of secondary growth like hardwoods. For this reason, palms do not increase their trunk diameter as they grow taller like other trees.

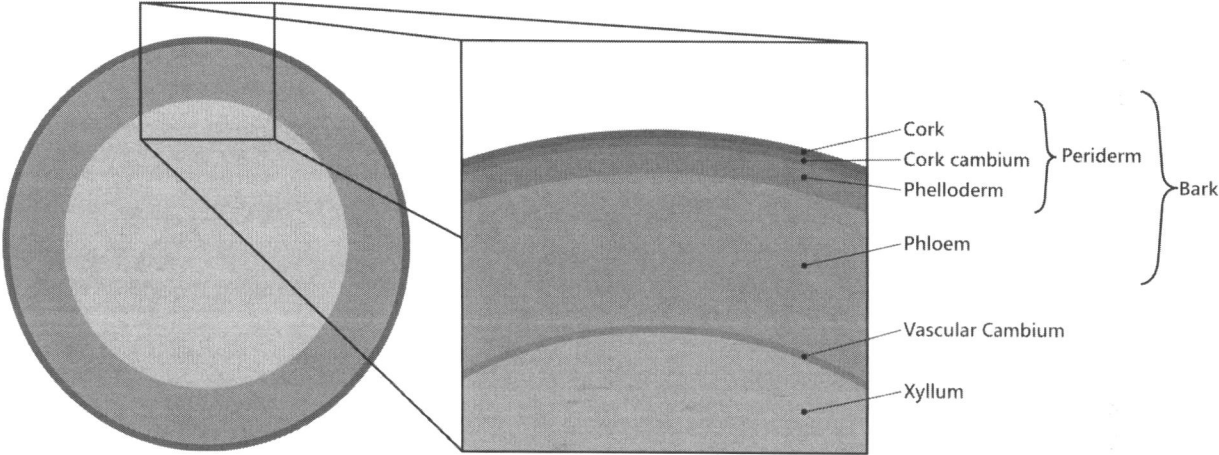

DIFFUSE POROUS AND RING POROUS TYPES

Ring-porous trees such as oaks (Quercus) create different-sized vessels, or water conducting cells, at different times in the growing season. Wood produced in the springtime, or early wood, will have larger-diameter vessels than late wood that is formed towards the end of the growing season. **Diffuse-porous trees** like Afzelia (Afzelia spp.) will form similar-sized vessel cells throughout the growing seasons. Sapwood refers to living layers of xylem cells nearest the cambium and can vary with thickness among tree species. Additionally, ring-porous trees are the only type to produce true heartwood, while diffuse-porous trees will form false heartwood of discolored inner xylem.

DORMANCY

Hardwood trees change colors in the fall as the **chlorophyll** in their leaves begins to break down and allows for other chemical pigments like carotenoids, flavonoids, and anthocyanins to come on display. As hormones in a tree trigger the formation of a **chemical barrier** between the stem and leaf petiole, that creates a brittle connection, allowing the leaf to drop. Some trees, such as beeches (Fagus sp.) and some juvenile trees will hold on to leaves late into the dormant season, while other types of trees will fail to form **abscission zones** when they are stressed.

Roots

Roots that grow along the soil line are known as **lateral roots**. Roots that grow outwards and then straight down are called **sinker roots**. Some trees begin life with a **tap root** that grows directly downwards from the seed, but most lose this feature by the time they mature. **Oblique roots** will grow at a 45° angle downwards to assist in the anchoring of the tree. **Fibrous roots** consist of a root cap which covers the expanding meristematic tissues beneath. Behind the meristem is the region of elongation, where growth occurs; followed by the region of differentiation, where root hairs diverge out at 90° from the parent root.

Leaves and Transpiration

Plants pull water up to their leaves from roots through a passive force created between leaves and water-conducting **xylem cells**. Water assists with the processes of **photosynthesis** and is released through stomata during the respiration of plant cells. **Stomata** prevent the excess loss of water during hot or dry periods by controlling the size of the stomata openings. **Guard cells** will respond to environmental conditions to regulate the size of the openings and will close if inadequate water is supplied to leaves. As transpiration slows, leaves will lose **hydraulic pressure**, known as turgor pressure, and begin to wilt.

Biomechanics

Mechanical

Mechanical damage, especially that created by human behaviors, can be damaging to trees in ways that do not exist in nature. Trees have not adapted to injuries such as soil trenching or repeated heading cuts. These types of **mechanical abuses** will generally lead to heavy stress for the tree and possibly initiate decline. Any time that trees are cut or damaged in a way that internal wood is exposed, there is the possibility for infection by fungal pathogens. Large wounds to trees require large amounts of energy to repair, and older specimens may not have resources available to fight off infection following severe damage.

Wound Effects & Response

The **first wall of CODIT** prevents the travel of rot upwards and downwards within the tree. The **second wall** prevents the rot from moving inwards towards the heart of the tree. The **third wall** utilizes the ray cells that grow from the center of the tree, like bicycle tire spokes, to prevent rot from encircling the trunk. The final wall to form is **wall 4** and consists of the creation of a reaction zone that closes off the wounded area and forms callus wood. Wall 1 is the weakest while wall 4 is the strongest barrier against the spread of decay. It is also very important that wall 4 not be damaged during pruning operations.

Pruning

General Principles of Pruning

GENERAL PRINCIPLES OF PRUNING

Pruning is conducted to improve the structure and discourage the growth of mechanically weak branches and trunks. Trees can be pruned to allow for human activities, such as raising a canopy to allow for mowing and to open vista views around trees. Trees are also pruned to remove dangerous tree parts and to reduce the risk of failure. Additionally, trees can be pruned to encourage fruiting or flowering in some species, and to create better airflow and light conditions. Pruning **young trees** is a good practice because it can prevent structural problems later in life, and young trees will compartmentalize wounds more effectively than mature trees.

BRANCH COLLAR

The branch collar is the place where trunk and branch wood diverge, forming a mechanically supportive union that holds the weight of the branch. Healthy **branch collars** will have a gradual taper away from the trunk and a branch bark ridge that forms an equal and opposite angle from the branch attachment angle. Where the collar stops rapidly tapering is considered the optimal spot to make pruning cuts because it is where the chemical barrier called the **branch protection zone** will most effectively wall off decay when a pruning wound is created. If a tree union is **codominant**, it will generally lack a defined collar and branch bark ridge.

INCLUDED BARK

Included bark is generally found in **codominant unions** where tree fibers have split into two leaders without formation of a branch collar. Bark from the codominant branches or trunks is squeezed together at the union and can create a **structurally weak area** that is prone to failure. Unions that have a tight V-shaped crotch and a tight angle of attachment will be prone to included bark problems. Early on in tree life, it may be possible to reduce or remove codominance, but as a tree matures, it may be more difficult to fix these problems and cabling and bracing may be required in instances where pruning would be ineffective or detrimental to tree health.

EFFECTS OF TIMING

Generally, it is better to prune most types of trees in the late winter or early spring prior to **bud break**. This gives the tree the most potential for compartmentalizing wounds by having the entire growing season to repair itself. Pruning late in the season will leave the wound open for the entirety of winter, where **desiccation and fungal pathogen establishment** can occur. Trees and shrubs grown for fruit production or flowering may have different timing considerations based on when they form flowering buds. It is important to try and avoid pruning right at the time of bud break because trees are physiologically vulnerable during this time and bark will "slip" as the **vascular cambium** begins to expand during spring flush.

FLOWER FORMATION

Flowering trees and shrubs that form flowers on previous year's growth, such as apples (Malus) and pears (Pyrus), should be pruned **after flowering or fruiting** to prevent the removal of new buds. Trees forming flowering buds on current year growth, such as Beautyberry (Callicarpa), should be pruned in the **dormant seasons**. It is important to remember that some trees, like apples, may form flowers on 2- or 3-year-old stems based on their cultivar, and require special pruning techniques. Another consideration for planning pruning activities is the prevalence of certain **pathogens or pests** that may be more prevalent during certain times of the year. Consult your local extension office or reputable literature prior to pruning if you encounter a species or cultivar you are unfamiliar with.

Techniques

Collar Cuts

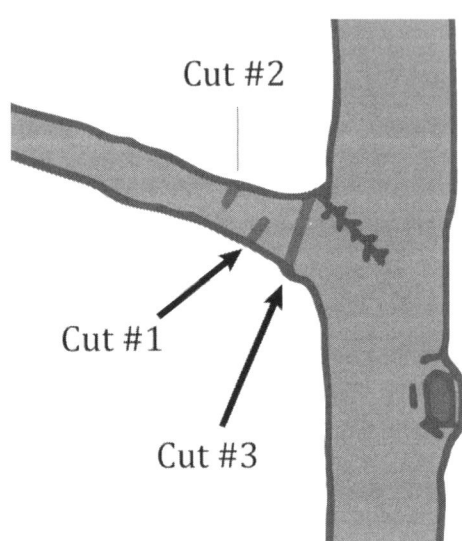

The **3-part cut** is an effective way to remove tree branches without causing unnecessary tearing of bark and wood fibers and will prevent damage to the **branch protection zone** found within the branch collar. The first cut severs the compression wood on the underside of the branch, while the second cut will cause the branch to pop off as the tension wood is severed. This is done a few inches out from the collar, so that a small stub is all that needs to be removed to complete the cut. If a **chainsaw** were used to make this style cut, the second cut would be placed slightly closer to the trunk, so that the chainsaw bar does not become pinched in the kerf of the cut.

Heading Cuts

Heading cuts are pruning cuts that do not result in reduction or subordination to an adequately sized lateral branch. Also known as **topping**, this practice causes extreme watersprout production, and can lead to internal decay of branches and trunks that are unable to compartmentalize these large misplaced wounds. Trees that have been topped can be more vulnerable to wind throw and fail unexpectedly as decay extends downwards into the tree. **Restoration pruning** for previously topped trees includes management of watersprout growth and removal of dead or dangerous branches.

Reduction Cuts

Reduction cuts are used to shorten leaders and branches in a way that the tree may effectively manage the wound and prevent excess watersprout production or branch dieback. A **reduction cut** is made directly above a lateral branch that is at least 1/3 the diameter of the parent stem. The lateral will then assume apical control as the wound is compartmentalized. If the new leader is too small or large, the tree may fail to compartmentalize the wound or form numerous watersprouts. Different tree ages and species will respond to reduction cuts in different ways. Young, vigorous trees will generally accept reduction cuts more readily than older trees with sluggish growth.

Pruning Tools and Their Application

Hand pruners are best used for branches up to 3/4 of an inch and should be the *bypass type*, not the *anvil type* that are used for roses and other cane-producing shrubs. Cuts between 3/4 and 2 inches should be made with **loppers**, as these tools will be able to deliver the cleanest cut for branches of this size. Cuts over 2 inches should use a **hand saw** or **pole saw** to make a cut. Any branches over 3-4 inches in diameter should be made with a **chainsaw** by qualified personnel. Selecting the correct tool for pruning cuts will minimize fatigue and prevent unnecessary damage to bark and branch collars.

Types of Pruning

Cleaning

Crown cleaning is a type of pruning aimed at removing all the dead, dying, defective, and diseased branches within a tree crown. Removal of **dead branches** reduces the risk of branch breakout that could injure people or break property located near the tree. Dead wood may also harbor insects or serve as a "court of rot" whose presence may encourage further infection of living branches. **Crossing or rubbing branches** may also be removed to improve the structure of the tree, depending on the scope and objectives of the pruning. Never will more than 25% of the **live crown** be removed in one season, as this can be detrimental to tree health. Larger and older specimens may realistically not be able to tolerate even 25% reduction in crown volume, so adjust this value as necessary when pruning mature trees.

Reduction

Reduction pruning aims to shorten the height or length of a tree or tree part. **Reduction cutting** is commonly conducted to prevent breakout of overextended or damaged branches, to make room for a manmade structure, or to maintain a tree or shrub in a smaller state as an ornamental or fruit producer. Reduction pruning should always employ **proper reduction cuts** that subordinate removed leaders back to a branch that is at least 1/3 the size of the removed branch. Trees are regularly reduced under powerlines and near buildings to prevent damage to lines and possible energization of the tree. In some exceptional conditions, it is acceptable to make **heading cuts** to prevent the total loss of the tree, or in overly mature trees where a large wound would be more detrimental than the heading cut.

Thinning

Thinning is a practice that has recently lost recognition as an acceptable practice by ANSI A300 standards due to the overapplication and misapplication of its practice. **Thinning** is the removal of a certain percentage of small diameter material to increase **light infiltration** and **airflow** in the crown. It was found that aggressive or continual thinning was resulting in the "lions tailing" of branches that increases the risk of failure and can lead to sun damage on bark. Thinning is still utilized in **orchards** and with trees that have been damaged by **topping**, and the judicious use of this technique may still have a place in certain applications.

Raising

Crown raising aims to increase the level of open space underneath the live crown of a tree. This is generally conducted to make room for **human activity**, and to prevent **damage to lower branches** on the tree. Some common applications of crown raising would include the removal of lower branches that hang into roads, impede traffic, obscure line-of-sight near intersections, and to prevent damage of branches that may be struck by large trucks. Crown raises are also employed to allow for activities like lawnmowing and to give space for understory plants. **Excessive crown**

raising can, in some cases, create instability that leaves trees growing in exposed areas more vulnerable to failure during storms. Consider the specific site conditions and species failure profile prior to conducting a crown raise.

VISTA PRUNING

Vista pruning is the removal of tree parts to create a **visual corridor** for human sight and is commonly conducted to improve the view of distant objects or landscapes. Vista pruning, when correctly applied, will make use of **directional and reduction pruning** to maintain tree health, while avoiding techniques like heading cuts and lion tailing. If the arborist believes that the pruning will overly damage or destabilize the tree, they should consider different options, including removal and replacement with a more suitable species. Some localities have special **tree ordinances** that regulate vista and other types of pruning, so check with local government requirements before recommending pruning.

RESTORATION

Restoration of a tree crown is generally conducted to help repair tree crowns damaged in storms, or by human activities including vandalism and poor pruning practices. When trees have been damaged through topping, they will generally develop large numbers of **watersprouts** from latent buds in the trunk. Watersprouts with poor attachment and excessive growth rates should be removed or reduced. Watersprouts growing directly below the heading cut should be limited to 2 or 3 in number, selecting the ones with the best growing form and attachment angles. The climber should also inspect the crown for **decay** and establish a regular **pruning cycle**, as restoration generally requires several iterations to accomplish canopy revitalization.

PRUNING PALMS

Palms lack branches and instead have **fronds**, large leaves held to the trunk by a slender **petiole** or leaf stalk. Fronds can become very long and heavy on some species of palms and, when they break free, can injure pedestrians and cause damage to structures. Arborists should generally avoid removing **living fronds** and should take special care when removing **dead fronds**. Every year a tree worker is killed by asphyxiation or crushed when fronds of large palms collapse onto a climber. Fronds should always be pruned from the top down, and removal of anything between 90° and vertical should be avoided. **Hurricane cuts**, or skinning cuts that remove unnecessary amounts of foliage or damage the trunk, should also be restricted.

PRUNING TOOLS

Contaminated pruning tools can promote the spread of infectious tree pathogens between trees and even branches on the same tree. **Bacterial leaf scorch** and **fire blight** are examples of pathogens that can be easily spread by contaminated pruning shears or saws. Use a **diluted beach solution** to clean tools and become aware of **local plant diseases** in your area and what times of the year infection is most likely. Avoid these times and making cuts unless absolutely necessary on vulnerable species.

POLLARDING

Pollarding is an old pruning technique that uses **internodal (heading) cuts** made to young trees, generally in urban areas to limit their height and create a visual effect. Heading cuts are made early in the tree's life, before it begins growing heartwood, and maintenance cuts on the pollarded branches are maintained throughout the life of the tree. **Topping** often is conducted on older wood and does not generally come with the promise of continual maintenance. When pollarding, the initial cuts should come within the first $1/10^{th}$ of the tree's life. Afterwards, no more heading cuts are to be made on the tree. Certain tree species can be readily pollarded while others may not accept this type of pruning.

ESPALIER

Espaliers grow in areas limited in space and light to maximize production of flowers and fruit of certain types of trees. Walls, fences, and trellises are areas where espaliers are typically grown, and trees are tied and trained to wire or wood structures to encourage a **two-dimensional growth pattern**. Annual pruning and maintenance is generally required for this type of ornamental pruning. Vines and some cane-producing plants such as roses are also trained in this manner and formal and informal versions of this type have been employed for many centuries.

WOUND DRESSING

Wound dressing was used for many years and was said to improve the healing of wounds and to prevent internal decay. Research has found that most of these claims were unfounded and allowing the tree to heal by its own means was just as effective. Wound dressings are still utilized in trees susceptible to **oak wilt**, discouraging insects that carry the disease from being attracted to open wounds on the tree. If a wound must be treated with a wound dressing, ensure that is a **non-phytotoxic substance**, or those that do not cause death to plant tissues.

DIRECTIONAL

Directional pruning is a practice whereby branches are encouraged to grow away from or towards an obstacle or area. Directional pruning is often used in **vista pruning** and in **utility pruning** to encourage a tree or tree branch to grow away from powerlines. Proper pruning cuts should always be made a consideration to the long-term stability of the tree. If a greater hazard will be created through directional pruning, then other options should be explored.

SUBORDINATION

Branches that are demonstrating an undesirable level of **apical dominance** or are **codominant** to the central leader in a tree, should be considered for **subordination**. A cut will be made directly above a lateral branch that is of adequate diameter to take over dominance after the removal of the main stem. The result should re-establish the apical dominance of the main leader and allow for the pruned branch to continue growing in a more controlled manner. If a tree requires a large amount of material to be subordinated, it is generally better to do it over the course of several pruning cycles to avoid removing over a quarter of the foliage.

Utility Pruning

PURPOSE

Line clearance arborists and trainees are trained in the special techniques and protocols for working near energized conductors. They are employed or hired contractually by the power company and have a direct line of communication to personnel managing the power grid. Line clearance arborists will also have the special tools and equipment to work near powerlines and other conductors. **Utility arborists** are generally trained on how to make proper pruning cuts, but also have the liberty to make heading cuts if necessary, to maintain the utility corridor.

TECHNIQUES

The **minimum standoff distance** for a non-certified arborist is *10 feet* for any conductor. As energized conductors increase in voltage, a higher standoff distance should be determined based on tables provided by ANSI. Qualified **line clearance arborists** have their own tables of minimum standoff distances that they observe. **Altitude** also plays a part in standoff distances, so a climber should know roughly how high they are. It should be assumed that any energized conductor holds a lethal dosage of electricity, and that trees, vines, or tools can become energized if they contact an energized line.

Recognizing Industry Standards and Best Management Practices

ISA

The **International Society of Arboriculture** is an international nonprofit organization that promotes the practice of tree care by qualified professionals. The ISA provides training resources and conducts testing-based **certification programs** for arborists in a wide range of tree industry sectors. The ISA also manages several **publications** that promote research and training initiatives within the world arboriculture and urban forestry. The ISA sets standards for ITCC **tree climbing competitions** and promotes local chapter climbing events. Resources for tree owners to find qualified arborists and make informed decisions about tree maintenance are also made available by the ISA.

TCIA

The **Tree Care Industries of America**, like the ISA, helps arborists and tree care companies get the information and training they need to work within industry standards of safety and tree care. TCIA has several **performance-based certifications** available and a rigorous **accreditation program** for companies that meet the highest standards in the industry. TCIA also provides statistical data on accidents that occur as a result of arboricultural work and list recent accidents and fatalities on their website.

ANSI/CSA

ANSI (**American National Standards Institute**) and the CSA (**Canadian Standards Association**) are non-government organizations that establish standards for **safe working procedures** for tree work and other hazardous occupations. ANSI is composed of a committee of expert industry professionals who meet and decide upon best practices and policies that they feel are necessary to prevent injury to tree workers. These **regulations** may then be adopted by state governments, companies, and other organizations as standardized work practices. All arborists should be familiar with **ANSI Z133**, the document that outlines all tree work safety practices in the United States.

OSHA

OSHA, or the **Occupational Safety and Health Act**, is a government organization in the United States that enforces safe working practices. OSHA differs from ANSI in that it has the ability to use **penalties and fines** to ensure compliance of rules and regulations governing jobsite safety. Arboricultural work is regulated through **29 CFR**, a document written and periodically updated by OSHA that incorporates many aspects of the ANSI Z133 standards. Specific standards for a whole host of different arboricultural practices are covered by various subheadings under the 29 CFR, such as subpart **1910.266**, which governs all logging operations. In Canada, a similar government body known as **CanOSH** dictates policy and enforcement of safe work practices.

Diagnosis/Treatment

Plant Health Care

DIAGNOSTICS

The **plant diagnostics process** is a procedure for analyzing conditions and factors that contribute to plant disorders and making educated recommendations to improve the health of a landscape plant. Diagnostics take into consideration the species, history, environmental and cultural factors, and how they impact plant health. **Biotic disorders** are those that are caused by a living organism such as an insect or fungus. **Abiotic disorders** are those that are caused by non-living factors such as rainfall and soil conditions. A successful diagnostician will have a broad understanding of plant types and the biotic and abiotic disorders prevalent in their area.

STRESS

Stress factors are conditions that are unfavorable to tree growth and, either by themselves or in tandem with other stressing factors, may lead to the decline and ultimate death of a tree. If a tree suffers from **soil compaction** leading to a lack of air in its root zone, the tree may display dieback in the canopy. If this tree becomes further stressed as a result of drought or infestation of leaf chewing insects, it may go into **decline** and ultimately die. Some stressing factors may not be evident until the tree is in very poor condition, which is why it is important to regularly **inspect** high value landscape trees for early signs of stress.

SIGNS AND SYMPTOMS

Signs include any definitive remnants or physical evidence that has been active on or near a plant. Frass (boring dust from bark beetle activity), mushrooms, conks growing from the stem or roots of a tree, and egg cases laid on a leaf would be included under a list of signs. **Symptoms** refer to observable responses to pests or pathogens that the plant may display. Crown dieback, chlorosis, excessive watersprout production, and trunk bleeding could all be considered symptoms of an underlying disorder. Diagnosticians should consider all signs and symptoms and gather an accurate **plant history** before trying to determine a cause and possible solution for the disorder.

LEAF DISORDERS

Bacterial leaf scorch is a common disorder that will show up as blotchy necrosis that appears as if the leaves in part of the crown have been singed. It is caused by bacteria that attacks the xylem of twigs and branches in oaks and other trees and can eventually lead to tree death. **Leaf blotch** appears as blistered or raised areas of discolored tissue on leaves and is generally caused by fungal infections following a wet spring season. **Leaf galls** display as raised areas of dense, swollen tissue on leaves that can sometimes be brightly colored. They are caused by a variety of organisms, including parasitic wasps and mites. **Vascular wilting** can be caused by drought or a number of pathogens that disable or destroy water-conducting tissues in the trunk and branches.

Diagnosis, Procedures and Techniques

EMPLOY TECHNIQUES TO IDENTIFY

When attempting to identify a pest or pathogen, sometimes referred to as a **causal agent**, it is important to first correctly **identify** the plant, including the species and specific cultivar you are examining. Compare the plant to other plants of the same species that may be growing nearby.

Oftentimes, entire stands of trees will be affected by the same disorder. Take note of the **surroundings**, including any changes in grade or drainage, and determine whether the signs and symptoms are displayed evenly throughout the plant or if it is affecting only one half of the crown, older foliage, etc. **Foliage** is a good indicator for tree vigor and health and should be closely observed for damage or signs of disease. Finally, inspect the **root crown** and **base** of the tree for signs of fungal activity, mechanical damage, or other root disorders.

OBSERVATION AND HISTORY

Gathering a detailed **site history** from the client or tree owner can oftentimes reveal the source of the condition and give an idea for how gradual or rapidly the problem is advancing. Consider asking the tree owner about **environmental and cultural conditions** that may have changed during the course of the tree's life, as these factors are generally the cause of urban tree death. Oftentimes, tree owners will focus on one specific aspect of the tree and it may be helpful to ask the same question different ways to determine an accurate site history. Once site history is determined, it may be possible to extrapolate if the condition will improve or decline in the future and formulate a plan for treatment.

TREE STRESS

Oftentimes a tree disorder will be a result of **biotic (living) causes**, such as a fungus or insect that is taking advantage of a weakened tree suffering from an underlining abiotic condition. **Abiotic conditions** include any factor that is from a non-living cause, such as drought, soil compaction, or extreme temperatures. A **complex** refers to the combination of all the factors affecting tree health and development. Sometimes **causality** is given to only one agent rather than the myriad of different factors that are contributing to a problem. Important also to consider is whether a stressor is chronic or acute in nature. **Chronic conditions** refer to a continuous activity or component of stress, whereas **acute stressors** are from a single event, such as trenching conducted through a tree's root zone.

SOIL CONDITIONS

City soils are often highly compacted and lack adequate space for tree growth. Most trees that die before becoming established suffer from some sort of water deficiency or excess. pH problems are also responsible for nutrient unavailability problems and certain trees, such as palms, are particularly susceptible to nutrient deficiencies in depleted urban soils. When diagnosing a problem in the **urban environment**, consider the effects of pollution and if de-icing salts may be accumulating in the root zones of trees. Other toxic chemicals may also be present in urban soils along with plastics and building debris that can become an obstacle to root growth.

WEATHER DAMAGE

Sunscald is a problem in cold climates where trees are exposed to below-freezing nighttime temperatures. When the warming rays of sunlight strike the trunk and branches in the morning, it sometimes causes cracking that can reoccur annually. **Frost cracking** occurs as a result of rapid temperature drops that results in unequal expanding and contracting that can injure the trunk. Damage from **snow loads and ice** is another problem that can affect most or all of the trees in an area and cause power outages and road obstruction. Damage from **high winds** can result in damaged trees and whole tree failures when roots are pulled up from the ground. Finally, **lightning strikes** affect exposed trees and those living on hilltops, and trees struck by lightning will exhibit longitudinal scars that often travel the entire height of the tree.

Insect, Nematodes, Diseases and Mites

BIOTIC DISORDERS

Damage from biotic, or living, factors will generally not appear uniformly throughout a tree or group of trees as the effects of an abiotic stressor would. **Biotic disorders** may show evidence of feeding, such as chewing by insects or larger animals like deer and rabbit. Signs of animal reproduction might also be evident in the case of nests or egg casings that may be present on the tree. Some plant-feeding insects and mites are so small that they may not be visible and only indirect signs and symptoms may indicate their presence. **Mechanical damage** to branches and trunks can be from both living and non-living sources, so gather information on local vertebrate species and their habits. Sapsuckers and woodpeckers can be particularly damaging to certain trees and shrubs because the holes that they create can be infected later by fungal pathogens. Biotic stressors are oftentimes caused by **multiple pests** that have a symbiotic or parasitic relationship with each other.

PIERCING/SUCKING/RASPING

Leaf miners feed on the phloem of leaves by tunneling between the upper and lower cuticle to extract the nutrient-rich tissues located here. Other insects will only eat the leaf tissues between the veins and are known as **leaf skeletonizers**. Aphids and psyllids generally have sucking mouthparts that allow them to drain liquids from the plant leaves after they pierce into it, like a hypodermic needle. Borers are generally the larval state of beetle species and will tunnel beneath the bark or into the heartwood of trees, in some cases causing serious damage to the cambium of trees. Nematodes and weevils will feed on roots of plants, making them difficult to find without laboratory analysis. It is important to realize that insects may pass through several different life stages before reaching adulthood and may feed on different parts of the plant in each life stage.

CHEWING

Chewing insects are oftentimes moth or butterfly **larval stages** (caterpillars) that feed on leaves until they enter a pupal state. Gypsy moths and cankerworms are major problems in different parts of the country and can sometimes totally defoliate a tree when their populations become numerous. Most healthy deciduous trees can accept some defoliation from insects, but if attacks continue year after year, the cumulative effects can lead to decline. Sawflies and weevils will sometimes eat the needles of conifers, but most chewing insects are found on **hardwood species**. There are numerous pesticides available to kill chewing insects if they become too numerous, and certain bacteria, such as **Bacillus thuringiensis**, are effective in their control.

BORERS

Boring insects that attack the phloem and xylem are common throughout the world and are responsible for some of the most economically damaging tree disorders in existence. Emerald ash borer, Asian long-horned beetle, and a variety of pine-boring beetles are some of the major pests affecting trees and come from both native and exotic sources. Bark beetles are difficult to control once they are already present in the tree, and sometimes there are local laws governing the transportation and destruction of infected wood. **Holes** in the trunk from exiting adult beetles and the presence of **frass**, or wood shavings, is an indicator of boring insects. **Galleries**, or small maze-like tunnels, may be found under the bark or in the wood of infected trees and their shape can be indicative of specific species of boring insects.

GALLS

Galls can be caused by a number of different species including mites, insects, and bacterium. Mites are a type of arachnid and generally suck on leaves to acquire nutrients, while some are predators of other organisms. Eriophyid mites are common gall formers and will inject compounds into leaves and stems that can form into galls. Certain parasitic wasps are gall formers and will inject eggs into plant tissues to create a living egg sac to harbor their young. **Galls**, unless they are extremely numerous, will not kill trees and take on an interesting variety of different shapes, textures, and colors.

VECTORS

Vectors are organisms that are capable of transporting another pest or pathogen between hosts. **Vectors** in trees generally take the form of an insect that carries a fungus, bacteria, or virus on its body that then infects other trees as the insect seeks out other trees. **Oak wilt** is a vascular disease that is transported on two-lined chestnut borer beetles in the Eastern US. **Dutch elm disease** is also transported by bark beetle species and ambrosia beetles of various species, spreading xylem-staining fungus in a variety of trees. Vectors also include **birds** and other **vertebrates** that can transport fungal spores on their feathers or fur. Oftentimes, prevention of tree diseases is dependent on suppressing the vector species rather than the actual causal agent.

Diseases

DISEASE TRIANGLE

The disease triangle refers to the factors necessary for the infection of an organism by a pathogen. First, the **infectious agent** must be present in the environment before it can become established and begin to multiply. The **host organism** must also be susceptible to the disease. Entire populations or individual trees suffering from a complex of other problems may make a tree susceptible to a pathogen. Finally, the **environmental conditions** must favor the infection and establishment within the host organism. **Time** is an additional factor that may accelerate or inhibit the pathogen and can sometimes alter the severity of the disorder. Most diseases are host specific and will only infect one species or a small group of closely related species, though some, like Armillaria root rot, may infect a large variety of trees.

FUNGI

Fungi cause a wide range of disorders in plants, including leaf disorders such as spots, rusts, scabs, and vascular wilt disorders that destroy cambium and xylem cells. Some **fungi** attack living plant tissues while others can only grow on dead plant materials. Certain fungi are helpful to plants and are present in **mycorrhizal relationships** in the roots of trees. Trees die and break down by way of fungal decomposition and are made available to other trees when they become components in soil.

BACTERIA

Fire blight is a very infectious bacterial disease that affects a large number of fruit trees of the rose family, including pears, apricots, and pyracanthus. Fire blight is spread by insects and by using contaminated pruning tools. **Bacterial leaf scorch** affects oaks and other broadleaved species and can kill trees in a matter of a few seasons. **Crown gall** is another bacterial disease that causes knotty growths on the root crown of a broad range of trees and shrubs. Bacterial infections often manifest as tissues that seem like they have been soaked in water and often have a foul odor.

VIRUSES AND MYCOPLASMA-LIKE ORGANISMS

Viruses and **phytoplasma bacteria** are some of the simplest of living organisms and can be spread by insects and other animals that feed on tree parts. They usually have to come into contact with open wounds in trees before they can begin to colonize the host. Viruses are not aggressive killers of trees but can weaken and exert stress on infected plants. Some visual traits such as variegation, or light-colored stripes or mottling on plant leaves, is the result of a virus infection that is considered desirable, and variegated cultivars are often proliferated by grafting.

Abiotic: Physiological Problems, Mechanisms/Structure, Climate/Microclimate, Animal

POLLUTION

Pollution damage can usually be detected on the leaves of affected plants and will arise as discolored spots, chlorosis, interveinal necrosis, abnormal leaf curling, and a pale or silvery appearance. Effects of **phytotoxic** (meaning literally tree poison) chemicals sometimes are indistinguishable from biotic disorders, making pollution damage difficult to diagnose. Gathering information on any activities involving pesticides or other chemical applications near the growing site may reveal clues on the cause of the disorder. **Herbicide drift** from nearby farms or applications on turf are many times a source of phytotoxic chemicals. Herbicide damage will often improve if the damage is not severe, and special attention should be paid when applying herbicides in proximity to trees and shrubs.

CLIMATE

Trees that are planted outside of their native range may be more susceptible to **disorders** involving extreme heat or cold and may be more likely to suffer from **water deficit**. Trees from arid environments may do poorly in humid environments due to increased susceptibility to fungal and bacterial pathogens that they are not exposed to in dry climates. Still, some trees will strive outside of their native range but may just demonstrate a different growth habit or grow smaller or larger in a new environment. Worldwide, there are many trees that will grow invasively outside of their native range, and some trees are illegal to plant in certain areas for this reason. Local government **rules and regulations** concerning exotic plant species should be consulted prior to considering introducing a new tree species.

ANIMAL

Browsing by **deer** will be evident by chewed leaves and buds located in the lowest part of the canopy and can sometimes be severe. Male deer will also rub bark off the trunks of small trees with their antlers during the fall rut. **Squirrels** often feed on the new buds of trees in the spring and will sometimes feed on the bark of thin-barked trees when food sources are scarce. **Beaver** can girdle trees with circumferential chewing on the trunks of trees during the process of dam building. Furthermore, the construction of dams can kill trees when flooding occurs. Placing barriers around the base of trees may help prevent the mechanical damage caused by beaver.

PHYSICAL VS. PHYSIOLOGICAL DISORDERS

Physical injury to trees includes any type of damage that destroys exposed and unexposed tissues by way of mechanics, heat, or other phenomenon whereby tree tissue is removed or killed. Physical damage usually stems from a single event, such as cutting of roots with a trenching tool or low branches on a street tree broken from passing trucks. **Physiological disorders** generally take a long time to develop, such as nutrient deficiency and seasonal damage from hard frosts. It is important to realize that physical and physiological disorders differ from pathogens and pests that are caused by biotic factors, though they can both be equally destructive.

ALLELOPATHY

Allelopathy is the release of chemicals by the roots of certain plants to kill or slow the growth of **nearby plants**. The effect of this is to reduce the competition for light, water, and nutrients of the allopathic plant. **Walnut** (Juglans) and **acacia** (Acacia) trees are known for being highly allelopathic and can exude phytotoxic substances from their roots that prevent the germination or growth of other plants. Allelopathy is sometimes selective and will only affect certain other plants or types of plants. In the example of the she-oak (Casuarina sp.) the decomposition of dead wood is what causes the release compounds toxic to other plants.

Treatment

PLANT HEALTH CARE

Plant health care (**PHC**) is a philosophy that takes into consideration the **full spectrum** of factors that play into the growth and development of plants, rather than focusing on problems when they appear. By seeing to the cultural or human behaviors on and around trees from a young age, you can reduce the likelihood or severity of tree health problems later down the line. Plant health care principles teach that **pesticides** should only be used as a last resort and should be applied judiciously and according to all labels and recommendations. **Monitoring** for pests and other disorders is also an important aspect of PHC as early detection is often necessary to prevent tree decline.

VITALITY VS. VIGOR

Vitality refers to the way a plant grows in its environment and can determine aspects such as mature height, crown spread, or annual incremental growth (twig elongation). **Vigor**, on the other hand, deals with the inherent genetic disposition of a plant and its ability to deal with environmental stressors, such as how a plant responds to short growing days or extended drought period. Arborists are mainly concerned with improving factors of vitality, while plant breeding and selection are the only areas where they can control vigor. **Resource allocation** is how plants divert energy resources to various processes as a response to environmental factors. For example, some trees when they are heavily stressed will produce massive crops of fruit in a last-ditch effort to reproduce before death.

TREE DEFENSE MECHANISMS

Lignin and **cellulose** are the building blocks of much of trees' woody structure. These compounds provide both the structural strength (lignin) and flexibility trees require as fixed organisms that cannot move, but still must protect themselves from mechanical damage. **Fungi** have developed chemical compounds that destroy cellulose, in the case of brown rots and lignin, as in white and soft type rots. Trees have developed further compounds to resist fungi that include phenols (tannins) and terpenes. Hardwood trees generally produce **phenols** to resist rot and feeding by herbivores, while conifers produce **terpenes** to protect their tissues. Some trees will allocate more resources to plant defense at the expense of growth rate, while others will grow quickly and sacrifice defense abilities.

INTEGRATED PEST MANAGEMENT

Integrated Pest Management (**IPM**) is a process whereby arborists view pests as parts of a complex system and apply treatments only when certain **population thresholds** have been achieved. Practitioners of IPM realize that client expectations and the potential for finding long-term solutions to pest problems must be balanced in order to make the most of scarce resources. **Client education** is an important part of IPM and allows the tree owner to make informed decisions about when and how to act when a pest enters the landscape. Pests will generally be present in all environments, but they may not reduce the aesthetic presence, functionality, or health of plants to levels that warrant immediate and drastic treatment. IPM also stresses the importance of employing a variety of cultural and organic methods to encourage tree health and pest resistance.

MONITORING

The three categories of information that should be gathered during plant monitoring include site information, plant information, and disorder information. **Site information** will include aspects such as climate, water resources, soil resources, and human activities such as foot traffic, mowing, fertilization, or construction. **Plant condition information** will include the species, growth rate, and the quality and quantity of foliage on the plant. **Disorder information** will include the specific pest or pathogen that is affecting the plant, how advanced is the disorder, and what options may be present for control of the given pest. **Action thresholds** determine at what level of pest infestation there should be a response. The conditions of the site, plant, and pest will determine if the action threshold should be changed. For example, if the pest has injured the plant to an extent that it will never recover, it will not be beneficial to begin costly treatment options.

DEGREE DAYS

Degree days are a method for describing and predicting the emergence of **specific pest populations** in temperate areas. A threshold for a degree day is generally set at **50°F** for most insect pests, and a calendar of the number of times that threshold is reached within the growing season will often determine when certain pests will arise. The time when trees will leaf out or flower can often be predicted using degree days as well. Local universities and extension offices will have calendars for degree day pest emergence that can be referenced by landscape managers. Monitoring and treatment action may need to be scheduled according to degree day calendars to ensure proper identification and management of certain pest species.

CONDITIONS FAVORABLE TO PESTS

Any time that a tree or other plant is **heavily stressed**, it will be easier for disorders to become established due to the reduction of plant defense resources, including chemical and physiological deterrents. **Excess plant debris** that can harbor insects and disease should be removed from the site. Sometimes excess plant material can produce overly wet or stagnant conditions that favor disorder establishment. Trees stressed by **drought** are far more likely to develop pest problems and pruning and transplanting should always be conducted in seasons that will best benefit the specific species and environment. **Pruning and transplanting tools** should always be sterilized prior to use and kept sharp to prevent unnecessary damage to roots and branch collars.

PEST MANAGEMENT GOALS

The main pest management goals include prevention, suppression, and eradication. **Prevention** is generally the most economically effective strategy and can be as simple as planting tree species that are resistant to local pests. Prevention requires consideration early on in the life of a tree or landscape and sometimes is inadequate when a new pest moves into an area. **Suppression** is a goal that works to lower the population levels of a pest to acceptable levels and to institute a monitoring program to determine if suppression tactics are working. **Eradication** is the least common goal merely because it is generally infeasible to eliminate every member of a pest population from an environment. Examples of situations where eradication is a warranted goal include eradication of rodents in a food facility, and an attempt to totally eliminate a new exotic species of insect before it gains a foothold in a new environment.

CULTURAL CONTROLS

Cultural controls include all aspects of plant management that can be regulated and improved by human activity. Selecting the right tree for the right hole and maximizing the soil, light, and water resources for the tree would be considered proper cultural practices for trees. Soil health is an extremely important aspect of cultural control; seeing that the proper levels of organic and mineral components are available in the soil will yield positive results for plants. **Cultural controls**, if instituted early in a plant's life, may be more effective than fertilization and pesticide usage, and are often less damaging to the surrounding environment than chemical control methods. Cultural control for this reason is an important extension of the **Integrated Pest Management**.

Biological Controls

Biological control agents make use of naturally occurring prey/predator relationships that exist in the natural environment. **Pathogens** such as *Bacillus thuringiensis*, a bacteria that damages the digestive tracts of chewing insects, would be considered a biological control agent that has been used with a great deal of effectiveness for controlling canker worms on hardwoods. When pest populations become too numerous, or overuse of biological control agents causes pests to form a resistance to the agent, it may become ineffective. Use of **wide-acting pesticides** may also reduce the levels of naturally occurring predator species in the environment that can lead to increased prevalence of pests. Pesticide use may be disallowed in certain areas or for certain applications, making biological and cultural control the only option.

Chemical Controls

Contact pesticides are applied directly to the trunk, branches, and leaves of the plant and are absorbed directly into plant tissues or kill insects or insect eggs that are on the outer part of the tree. These types of pesticides generally will have a fast reaction time as the chemical is placed directly onto the pest. The downside to contact pesticides is the **drift** that occurs as extra chemicals that have been broadcast into the air settles downwind from the application site. **Systemic pesticides** avoid this problem by being injected directly into the trunk of infected trees or applied to the root zone as a drench. These chemicals have a slower activation time as they require uptake by the tree's vascular system but avoid aerosolized drift. The downside to systemic pesticides can be the pollution of groundwater with excess chemicals.

Pest Resistance

Pests may become **resistant** or immune to pesticides when they are repeatedly used. For every pesticide there will be a certain number of naturally resistant members in a pest population. Repeated use will eliminate the susceptible members of the population, leaving the resistant ones to pass on their genes. After numerous application cycles, all or most of the pest population may demonstrate resistance to the particular pesticide being used. **Alternating** the use of pesticides with different modes of action can help prevent resistance. "Mode of action" refers to the way that the pesticide kills a pest, whether it attacks the nervous system, the digestive system, or affects how insect mouthparts function. Pesticide labels will indicate how many times a specific pesticide should be used, and how often it can be applied.

Alternatives to Pesticides

Many natural and organic options are available to plant managers who want to avoid the use of traditional pesticides. **Biorational control products** such as horticultural soaps and oils are effective for control of some pests and have a much shorter half-life in the environment than other pesticides. These products work by preventing gas exchange on the skin of insects such as aphids and scale insects and can be used repeatedly, though may cause damage to plants if over-applied. **Botanical insecticides** are naturally occurring plant compounds that effectively kill or resist insects that feed on plants. While these products are derived from naturally occurring sources, they may still be somewhat toxic, and all application and PPE requirements should be observed. **Insect**

growth hormones have also shown success in preventing pests by actively changing the reproductive capabilities of pests.

Urban Forestry

Benefits and Costs of Trees

URBAN FORESTRY VS. ARBORICULTURE

Urban forestry deals with the entirety of green infrastructure within a city and the upkeep of trees and vegetation on public and private lands within the built environment. **Arboriculture** deals more with individual trees and woody vegetation within a landscape and has a narrower focus than urban forestry. Within a city, there may be an entire team of people who work together for the benefit of the urban forest, including city foresters, planners, arborists, landscape designers, wardens and even volunteer tree boards consisting of concerned citizens. Arborists must be responsive to the specific needs and constraints of trees living in the urban environment, and aware of local planting and pruning guidelines that have been established in their area.

SOCIOLOGICAL

Studies involving trees' impact on human health and welfare have demonstrated that areas with **trees** will sometimes have lower crime rates, and residents tend to have an increased feeling of well-being and pride in their community. Trees have been found to improve recuperation rates of patients in hospitals with windows where they can view trees and reduce recidivism rates of criminals that have been incarcerated in areas surrounded by trees. Trees improve the property values of homes and commercial properties, and tree planting and creation of green infrastructure has been used to help elevate struggling urban communities. The **sociological and psychological benefits of trees** are evident by the popularity of green areas within cities.

ENVIRONMENTAL

Trees planted in the **urban environment** are helpful in the reduction of pollution and the cooling effects they have on roads and other hardscapes. Leaves and roots absorb pollutants and sequester carbon as they grow. Tree canopies and root systems slow the movement of storm water by slowing the velocity of runoff. This can improve the capacity of city wastewater systems and prevent flooding in some instances. **Urban heat islanding**, caused by heat retention on dark surfaces like roads and rooftops, is mitigated by a healthy canopy that absorbs sunlight. Areas that have high winds may also benefit from the windbreak effect that trees provide.

Appraisal and Valuation

TREE APPRAISAL AND VALUATION

Tree appraisal is conducted to determine the dollar value that is associated with urban trees by aggregating the various benefits they provide to a society through increased property value, energy savings, and pollution reduction considered along with maintenance and installation costs. There are many systems and formulas for the calculation of **tree value** with the **CTLA, or Council of Tree and Landscape Appraisers**, with the trunk formula method being one of the more popular tools. This method takes into consideration the trunk diameter, along with other factors including crown spread, location, and tree species. Finding the replacement cost of a large tree that is removed from a landscape is the most common reason for employing this type of tree valuation.

COMMUNITY TREE BENEFITS

Green infrastructure can be distinguished from **gray infrastructure**, or roads and buildings, in that it increases in value over time, rather than diminishing. As trees grow in size, so do their inherent benefits to people. Parks and other green areas provide places for people to recreate, and as population density increases, they become increasingly important as refuges for people and wildlife. Air and water resources benefit from the presence of areas where natural processes can occur, and economic and cultural sustainability are a result of well-maintained green infrastructure.

I-TREE

i-Tree is a computer program that allows tree managers to keep **detailed records** on all the trees within their jurisdiction and calculate value and make educated decisions on where plantings can take place and where maintenance may be required. Other programs allow citizen tree owners to upload data on their trees, which can then be viewed by the entire community. Advanced software platforms will allow city planners to integrate **GIS layers** that show where city trees are located with pertinent information on their condition, age, pruning requirements, etc. Some software will automatically create work orders and prioritize various input-based prerogatives based on user search criteria.

Regulatory and Legal Issues

LIABILITY ISSUES

Risk management, as it relates to urban forestry, includes the associated risks that trees pose to the public, tree professionals working within the urban forest, and the responsibility that the municipality undertakes as an owner of trees. Municipalities are sued on a regular basis throughout the country for failure to address risky situations created by trees. Along with branch and whole tree failure, pavement heaving and the creation of tripping hazards are some of the biggest litigation subjects surrounding city tree projects. Risk management planning is a necessary component of any municipal tree plan and may include record keeping of incidents and required training.

BEST MANAGEMENT PRACTICES

Best management practices are a set of standardized guidelines created by the **International Society of Arboriculture** that explain precisely how to conduct a wide range of tree care operations. Detailed information on how and when to prune trees, improve soil conditions, and even safety information such as wood chipper operations are covered in various BMPs. These documents are written by expert arborists with years of experience in the industry to ensure that the latest research-supported techniques are included in the BMPs. The popularity of these guidelines has led them to be adopted into organizational policies, making it important for arborists to have an understanding of them.

ORDINANCES

Tree ordinances are common in cities where the tree canopy has been cited as a significant asset and local governments look to maintain and improve trees growing on municipal and private lands. Ordinances institute standards for pruning, planting, and removal and oftentimes create a system of permitting and fines to enforce standards. Some examples of **tree ordinances** would include regulations that limit the removal of trees on steep slopes and prevent citizens from having trees topped. Tree ordinances may also create lists of **acceptable or preferred species** for new plantings and require new building permits to include provisions for tree plantings to offset heat and storm water runoff changes to the environment.

License and Permit Requirements

In many municipalities, in order to have a tree removed or pruned, it is required that a **permit** be applied for. Some permitting programs require that a municipal arborist make a site visit and approve the requested action. Some aspects of tree permits may be conditional in nature and require that certain criteria be met to stay in compliance with local regulations. **Pruning and planting BMPs** are often cited as required conditional aspects to permitting requests. Some municipalities require that tree companies wishing to operate in the city have an **ISA-certified arborist** on staff and may require monitoring programs by certified personnel following tree work.

Tree Preservation

Trees are important to cities because they reduce the effects of urban heat islands and slow runoff from storms. Trees add value to property and make communities with trees desirable to people to work and play in. Cities will sometimes establish **heritage tree programs** where citizens can apply to have large or otherwise unique trees added to a list maintained by the city. These heritage programs sometimes come with legal expectations to the maintenance of the tree, but often are a voluntary measure that hold no legal standing and tree owners may receive a plaque to identify the heritage tree. Other methods of tree protection include ordinances or **tree preservation orders (TPOs)** that legally protect individual trees or groups of trees in an area.

Street Tree Maintenance

Tree maintenance requirements will include both **regular maintenance** such as pruning, and **requests** created by citizens who have witnessed a failure or potential failure of city trees. For this reason, municipalities must be flexible in the way they prioritize maintenance issues. In recent years, many cities have moved towards **privatization** of tree care operations. The benefits to this approach include reduced legal liability and decreased costs as city benefit programs do not have to be extended to contractual employees. Problems associated with privatization include problems with monitoring private firms' performance and whether qualified contractors can even be found in an area. **In-house tree management** brings a higher degree of accountability and enhances the relationship between city governments and citizens.

Management

Site Assessment

Selection of **new planting sites** for city trees is important because placement of the wrong tree in the wrong place can lead to diminished success in young tree establishment and cause costly maintenance problems later. Trees should be planted in areas where they can be effectively nurtured through the establishment phase and will provide maximal benefits to the community in maturity. A set of priorities will be established for new plantings in a **master street tree plan**, and it is important that the city arborist ensure that the soil and other requirements are adequate for tree survival. Poor site selection can lead to dead trees that must be replaced and conflicts with utility and transportation infrastructure.

Tree Selection

Selection of tree species to be planted is dependent on the site factors at planting sites and the environmental conditions of the location. Each species comes with positives and negatives, and factors such as drought tolerance, shape of crown, and pollution resistance are all factors that should be considered before selection of new plantings. Trees that are not adequately adapted to their location will require more maintenance and live shorter lives than hardy, well suited varieties. Along with species, city arborists should select nursery stock that is of a **high quality** and have

qualified personnel present during acquisition of new trees to ensure that they meet selection standards.

Insects and Diseases

Monocultures, or plantings that consist of a single species, have been problematic to urban centers where introduced diseases and pests can become rapidly established. Dutch elm disease and emerald ash borers completely wiped out large numbers of trees for Midwestern cities in the United States, leaving entire areas bare of trees. One strategy for urban plantings to maintain diversity is the **10/20/30 rule**. This rule limits the planting selection include no more than 10% of any one species, 20% in one genus, and 30% in any single family of plants. Other strategies have gone farther to limit species selections to no more than 5%. Whichever strategy is adopted, proper diversity of plantings will reduce the chances and costs of a disease outbreak.

Wood Waste

Wood waste recycling is becoming an increasingly important issue for cities where dumping sites are limited, and in some cases, it has been made illegal to dispose of woody debris in landfills. **Firewood** is a common outlet of trunk wood, though wood smoke may become a serious pollutant in densely populated areas. **Composting** is an effective method to get rid of wood chips and utilizes microorganisms present in the environment to break down woody debris that can then be used for farming or integrated back into landscapes. Wood recycling is an important component of **LEED green building standards** and is continually becoming a standard goal of sustainable development practices.

Tree Inventories

Tree inventories will often work to improve safety issues associated with trees and can help to prioritize these issues. **Tree risk evaluations** are a component in maintaining a tree inventory and will help support work scheduling. The diameter, age, condition, and locations are other components that are tracked by tree inventories and can give helpful information on regular maintenance requirements of mature trees. **Tree and city infrastructure conflicts** such as damage to pavement and water or sewage pipes is another factor that may be documented in tree inventories and can be significant in tree placement and selection in the future.

Wildlife

Plants and animals living within cities are part of an **ecosystem** that is valued by many in the community and wish to see to their preservation. Some species and their nesting trees are **legally protected** and urban foresters should be aware of local species and the legal implications of their removal or suppression. Practices of eradication are being replaced with policies that try to improve and support the existence of a healthy environment for animals and people. **Wildlife refuges** within cities include parks and tree stands, and these areas are often destinations for citizens who have a great deal of appreciation for natural features. Arborists should consider how their actions will affect these natural communities and work to preserve and protect these resources.

Information and Education

Audience Types

Support networks such as volunteer tree commissions and boards are an important resource for urban foresters and can help inform the community about issues regarding urban trees. **Increased awareness** by citizens of their urban trees promotes the care and improvement of trees and concerned communities will make urban forest budgets a priority rather than an area for cuts when resources are limited. **Volunteer programs** that help to monitor and provide early care for new plantings have been successful in some areas and are known to cultivate a sense of pride and stewardship for trees among citizens. Engaging the community can also help to prevent and mitigate the negative effects of tree diseases that are affecting trees in the area.

DUTIES OF MUNICIPAL ARBORISTS

Municipal arborists are responsible for a multitude of responsibilities including management and supervision of staff and the planning, implementation, and monitoring of tree-related programs. City arborists are also responsible for maintaining a **budget** and defining terms of contracts if outside sub-contractors are utilized. Municipal arborists will also present **reports** to local government councils and collaborate with other city officials to streamline development and maintenance actions of infrastructure. Additionally, city arborists will set **performance measures** for tree-related programs and demonstrate accountability for achieving organizational goals. As leaders, municipal arborists must demonstrate qualities including technical competence, people skills, accountability, and good judgment.

Protection and Preservation

Protection

PLANNING/EVALUATION

Tree protection and preservation plans aim to maintain the health of existing trees and prevent injuries to tree roots, trunks, and branches. It is important to begin this process early on in project planning because it can take only one destructive action to kill an established tree. Heavy equipment driving over and/or burying tree roots when grading makes up some of the most common human activities which injure trees. A plan established to protect trees should prevent any construction activity from occurring within the root zone of trees by the creation of **physical barriers**. Mature trees are particularly vulnerable and may not be great candidates for tree protection if construction activities must be conducted within the dripline of the trees. Younger trees are able to adapt to changing conditions and are sometimes better candidates for tree preservation.

TREE PROTECTION ZONE

Tree protection zones (**TPZs**) should ideally extend out to the **dripline** of the tree and potentially farther in some instances. A guideline for determining the distance from the trunk is 1 foot for every inch of tree trunk diameter. For instance, a tree that is 20 inches in diameter should have a fence placed 20 feet from the trunk, creating a circular ring. Older trees and those that are more susceptible to construction damage may need this distance extended. **Mulching and weed suppression** within the tree protection zone is important to help keep roots well irrigated and free from competition. Arborists and planners should work together to ensure that TPZs are observed by construction workers.

LIMIT ACCESS

During the planning stage, it is important to establish **access routes** for the property where construction vehicles are allowed to enter and exit. Access routes will prevent unnecessary compaction of soil and damage to branches and tree trunks. If possible, compacted areas should correspond with parts of the property that will later house driveways, foundations, and utility pathways where soil is going to be **compacted or trenched** later. Areas where equipment is to be cleaned, such as concrete and painting devices, and where materials may be burned should also be located as far away from trees as possible to prevent pollution or heat damage to plant parts.

CONSTRUCTION TECHNIQUES

Tree wells consist of retaining walls that allow for the raising or lowering of soil grades around trees. Most of the absorbing roots of trees are located within the top few inches of soil. Preventing the burying or cutting of tree roots by creation of tree wells may be an effective preservation technique when construction must be conducted near trees. Larger tree wells are likely more effective than ones located directly beside the trunk. **Aeration systems**, including gravel and plastic piping, are sometimes used to allow roots to access air following grade changes, but are difficult to effectively implement. If **drainage patterns** near trees are drastically changed, tree wells and aeration systems may still be inadequate to ensure tree survival.

Damage

ROOTS

Soil must generally be compacted to a certain **bulk density** before permanent structures such as buildings and pavement can be constructed. Tree roots are unable to survive at such levels of compaction and will rapidly decline if even moderate amounts of root-containing soils are compacted. **Equipment** used for grading and compacting soil is extremely heavy; just driving it across a planted area can cause broken roots and overly compacted soil. If possible, use smaller and lighter equipment or hand tools in proximity to tree roots and, if roots must be travelled over, a combination of mulch and plywood sheets can be used to provide some protection for tree roots.

LANDSCAPE DESIGN AND TREES

Landscape designers that wish to utilize existing trees or groups of trees must consider practical implications of tree protection and the long-term requirements that may be necessary. By making small adjustments to the location of a building or sidewalk, **tree preservation efforts** may be more effective. If the protected tree is going to later create conflicts with the structure or be unacceptably costly to maintain, it should be addressed during the planning process to avoid unnecessary costs. Bridging concrete over root zones and tunneling under roots to run utility wires may be options for tree preservation but are extremely expensive to implement.

BRANCHES AND CROWN DAMAGE

The use of bulldozers and excavators near trees is a common source of damage to lower branches. Though these injuries may be compartmentalized by the tree, the initiation of rot from branches may continue into the tree trunk. This can be particularly damaging to trees that are already suffering root stress from building activities. Trucks may damage trees as they brush by, and construction workers will sometimes crudely prune trees to accommodate construction activities. Proper communication with contractors and establishment of physical boundaries such as **tree protection zones** are critical to the prevention of mechanical injuries to tree crowns.

DELAY IN CONSTRUCTION DAMAGE

Construction damage affects trees in many ways similar to natural causes, especially those associated with root disorders. Construction-damaged trees will often have sparse or yellowing foliage and dieback near the tips of branches. Excessive growth of water sprouts is also a common sign of construction damage, and injury to root crown will result in **basal decay** (butt rot). Early leaf drop or fall color is another indicator of construction-related stress. In trees that are suffering from water deficit, effects of construction damage may be evident within several days or weeks, but more often develops gradually as the tree declines over a series of years.

CHANGES IN EXPOSURE

When trees are removed from a forested area, it can be highly detrimental to nearby trees now living in **exposed conditions**. Damage from wind is the biggest factor for newly exposed trees, as trees growing together will have tall, thin trunks not adapted to living in the open. **Canopy blowout**, or whole tree failure from the roots, are common problems among newly exposed trees. **Understory trees** will also suffer from the removal of nearby trees which shaded their branches and root zone, leading to sunscald, frost damage, and water deficit as soil dries out. Pre-construction planning by qualified arborists and instituting a monitoring program are important to help prevent the effects of environmental exposure.

CONSTRUCTION SPECIFICATIONS

Construction specifications common in many European countries are now becoming more common in the US and other parts of the world to protect trees from the effects of construction damage. **Construction specifications** are laid out prior to breaking ground on building projects and establish rules and consequences for violating tree protection zones. Fines are instituted for violations and repeat offenders may be denied building permits for future projects. Remediation and replanting of trees to replace those that have been removed or damaged are also common requirements established in construction specifications. Heavy equipment operators and other construction workers should be informed of all tree-related concerns in writing prior to working onsite.

Post-Damage Management

ROOTS

Compaction is a very difficult problem to correct and damage to roots may be irreversibly damaged through construction activities. **Air excavation** through the use of an air spade or similar device is one option for remediation of compacted soil. Roots that have been damaged should be pruned with sharp, sterile tools to prevent the introduction of soilborne pathogens. **Vertical mulching**, or the drilling of large holes in the soil that are filled with loose and nutrient-rich soil, was once considered an effective technique for improving soil conditions but is becoming less common. **Radial trenching** using air tools in a sunburst pattern away from the trunk and backfilling with lightly amended native soil is a better option for soil remediation.

TRUNK

Damage from mechanical means generally will result in a permanent wound on the tree that will either compartmentalize by itself or become a hollow as decay advances into the xylem. **Bark tracing** is one option for mitigating the effects of wounds and entails the careful cutting of jagged, damaged bark surrounding the damaged area to create an even surface for callus wood to form along. If a piece of bark has come off cleanly from the trunk, it may be possible to re-apply the bark to the trunk to allow for the creation of a **bark graft**. Research has shown that this is very dependent upon the species, season, and the overall vigor of the tree. Bark grafts should be placed in exactly the same position they were, and a non-phytotoxic tape should be used to fix it in place.

CROWN

Damage from heavy equipment is similar to wind or ice damage and can leave trees unsightly and prone to infection from pathogens and boring insects. **Pruning** should aim to retain as much of the remaining canopy and focus on reduction or removal of entire damaged branches. **Cables or bracing hardware** may need to be installed in instances where structural stability of the tree has been compromised. As with all trees damaged during construction, braces and cables installed in trees will require continued monitoring and maintenance to ensure effective performance.

IRRIGATION AND DRAINAGE CONCERNS

Trees that have suffered from any degree of construction damage are likely to have **water deficit** problems in the future. Trees that did not sustain physical damage may also suffer as removal of companion trees and changes to light and drainage conditions can alter **soil moisture content**. Infrequent and deep **irrigation**, just as in new plantings, is recommended above frequent, shallow watering. The use of **tensiometers** or other soil moisture monitoring equipment may be helpful for determining an irrigation regimen. **Mulching** around damaged trees may also be an effective way to retain water in the root zone. Irrigation needs of trees following construction may be made simpler if designers are aware of plumbing considerations prior to final building design.

Arborist Responsibilities During Construction

An arborist's chief goal once construction has begun is to maintain and strictly protect **tree protection zones** and to ensure that **tree protection orders** are being maintained. Arborists will consider issues when changes are made to construction plans and communicate with superintendents and other staff about job site practices and tree injury. Finally, the arborist working with a public works department will see to the timely delivery of the finished product. A **monitoring plan** and long-term **PHC plan** should be established at the time of installment for all new landscapes surrounding buildings.

Tree Risk Management

Responsibility/Liability

DOCUMENTATION

Tree risk assessments are generally recorded on a standardized form made available for free by the ISA. These documents contain pertinent information such as a tree's scientific species, size, location, and a description of the surrounding area and any targets that may be affected by failure. The general environmental characteristics of the site, including prevailing winds and location of nearby trees, may also be helpful. History of the site is also an important aspect to record, including removal of nearby trees and details about any construction or cultural activities that have been performed on the tree. Risk ratings for entire trees or tree parts will also be recorded with options for mitigating potential failure.

NOTIFICATION

Arborists, through training and on-the-job experience, have a **duty of care** to act accordingly if they become aware of a risky situation posed by a tree. If an arborist is aware of a dangerous problem in a tree and that tree then fails, damaging property or injuring a person, the arborist may be found **negligent** in preventing the incident and could be held legally responsible for the damage or injury. If an arborist notices a blatantly risky situation, such as advanced decay in the crown of a tree, they should feel obligated to **inform** the tree owner and **record** the details of their findings to ensure that they are legally protected should the tree fail.

RISK ASSIGNMENT

Oftentimes, an arborist will be documenting risk assessments for a number of trees within a landscape. Consideration will be given to likelihood of failure along with the possible repercussions to structures and people. Different land owners will have different **risk tolerances** for various aspects of tree risk, and it is the responsibility of the arborist to assist in the creation of **priorities** for various mitigation options. There are a variety of formulas available to calculate risk and aid in the prioritization of different issues. The value of tree preservation will vary among different locations, but it is generally preferable over removal. If the tree is deemed to be overly risky and mitigation options cannot lower this risk to an acceptable level, then removal may be the only option.

Site Analysis

TARGET

A target has traditionally been identified as any person or piece of property that could potentially be damaged by a tree or tree part but has recently been extended to also include activities that may be disrupted as a result of tree failure. Targets will vary in significance when determining the overall **risk rating** for a specific component. For example, a playground outside of a day care center will be a much more important target to protect than a split rail fence along a road. **Mitigation of risk** to a certain target may be as simple as moving a picnic table out from under a tree containing large dead wood. It is important to consider all options when determining risk factors as they relate to targets.

SITE DISTURBANCE

As long-living organisms lacking the ability to move, trees are dependent on **growing sites** that remain stable and conducive to tree health throughout their lives. Small changes to soil, light, or water resources can have drastic effects, especially in mature trees. Arborists should examine the site to determine if any companion trees have been removed in recent history, or if any new man-made structures have been constructed in proximity to the tree. Trenching or pruning of roots is one of the most destructive practices near trees because it affects not only tree health, but also compromises the structural strength of the tree if supporting roots have been cut or killed. A healthy trunk flare is a good indicator of possible grade changes, and fungal pathogens in this area may indicate damage from human activity that could possibly be destabilizing.

Tree Risk Characteristics

DECAY/HOLLOWS/FUNGAL FRUITING BODIES

Trees suffering from **internal decay** may have obvious signs of fungal infection or none at all. The presence of **conks**, or tough, mushroom-like fruiting bodies on wood, are a sign of decay. Sometimes they will arise from the soil if they are growing from roots, and it is important to be able to distinguish these wood-feeding fungi from those growing from mulch or grass. **Hollows** can be open or closed and will always indicate decay. Closed hollows can be found by "sounding" the trunk with a rubber mallet and listening for changes in sound resonance. **Insects** such as carpenter ants, which live in soft wood created by decay, may signal significant internal rot. Finally, **nesting birds and other animals** may be utilizing hollow tree parts as habitat, so look for signs of associated wildlife living in the tree.

CRACKS

Cracks can be created by numerous factors but are generally a result of storm or ice damage, and different locations will have specific environmental factors leading to crack formation. **Hazard beams**, or vertical cracks on the trunks of trees, will many times be the result of root decay that has led to structural weakness and splitting of the trunk. **Transverse or lateral cracks** appear on branches, especially those that are excessively long and have little taper. These cracks are usually formed during high wind conditions, or as a result of snow loading. Cracks will often heal over and may fail later in life as decay is introduced into wood. **Horizontal cracks** on tree trunks are particularly dangerous, as it indicates the severing of longitudinal fibers in the wood that gives trees strength and flexibility.

BRANCH CONDITION

Strong branch structure is an important component in the way trees resist mechanical stress from environmental conditions. **Branch attachment angle** is generally consistent amongst a specific species and branch attachment angles that are overly acute or obtuse for that species may indicate a weak spot. Branches that are over 50% of the diameter of the parent stem are also an issue of concern, as they may have an increased chance of failure. Finally, branches that reach out much farther than other branches may indicate potential for failure in some trees. In general, trees with an open and well-spaced branch structure will have fewer problems with branch failure.

LEAN

Leaning in trees is not always a sign of structural weakness and many leaning trees will live as long as ones with straight trunks. Trees that have an uncorrected lean may be indicative of a tree that is currently failing due to a damaged **root plate**. Cracks in the soil or mounding on the side opposite the lean may indicate a failing root plate. Trees with a **corrected lean** will have a natural-looking crown that reaches upwards towards the light, whereas uncorrected leaning trees will look canted to one side. Trees with a corrected lean will also have a trunk flare that is thicker and broader on the side opposite the lean as the tree packs on more wood to support the uneven weight distribution.

Included Bark

Included bark generally occurs where branches join together in a V-shaped union. Bark becomes pinched between the two branches, making a weak junction that is prone to **splitting**. Co-dominant leaders on a tree will oftentimes form unions with included bark, and when a crack forms below areas of included bark, the risk of failure increases. **Decay** may appear in this area and is another condition that may further weaken the tree. Installation of **braces and/or cables** is a common method for reducing the chance of failure in trees with included bark. **Weight reduction** on one or both of the branches to reduce the load on the defect is another option for dealing with co-dominant stems.

Structural Root Damage

Damage or cutting of large **structural roots** close to the trunk is destructive in two ways. Not only is the tree potentially losing 15-25% of its fibrous root system, but the loss of large anchoring roots can **destabilize** the tree. Trees that have lost large parts of their root systems are prone to decay and are more likely to fail during storms. Examination of structural roots by way of **air excavation** is recommended for large trees in developed areas where major root damage is suspected. Monitoring and special attention to cultural needs will be necessary for all trees suffering large amounts of root damage.

Species History of Failure

Tree failure profile refers to the tendency of certain types of trees to fail in a similar fashion. Trees of the same species will tend to have the same structural problems and present similar risk factors. For example, the Bradford pear (Pyrus calleryana) has a strong disposition for branches with narrow angles of attachment with included bark. This problem is due to the genetic makeup of the tree and almost every Bradford pear specimen will fail at some point because of it. The species failure profile of a tree should always be considered when conducting risk assessments.

Lightning Injury

Lightning is a common abiotic factor that can heavily damage or destroy trees. Trees that are struck by lightning may not show signs for several years and factors such as bark thickness and texture can affect the level of damage inflicted. Trees that are struck by lightning are prone to **infestation** by insects and should be inspected and monitored for an increased chance of failure. Trees that are located on hilltops or growing in open areas are more prone to being struck by lightning. **Lightning protection systems** are an effective way to prevent lightning damage but are costly to install.

Edge Trees

Trees living in the margin area between forests and fields may represent an increased likelihood of failure. As **edge trees** grow towards the opening, they may develop an **unbalanced crown** that increases the chances of limb breakage or failure of the entire tree. If the opening in the canopy was created by land clearing with heavy machinery, it is also likely that edge trees have been damaged, further destabilizing their root system. Trees growing on the margins of forests are also prone to wind damage as they lack the natural windbreaks that trees growing in dense competition have.

BROWN ROT, WHITE ROT, AND SOFT ROT

Brown rot is a type of decay that generally affects conifers but is also present in some hardwoods. **Brown rot**, also known as brown cubical rot, gives wood a dark and burnt-looking appearance as the cellulose is digested by fungi, leaving only the brittle lignin behind. **Cellulose** gives trees the flexibility to move in the wind, and trees infected with brown rot have an increased risk of wind throw. **White rot** consumes the lignin in trees and leaves a spongy, light-colored substance behind as wood decays. Many **basal rots**, or decay isolated to the trunk flare of trees such as Ganoderma (artist's conk) and Armillaria (honey mushroom) are forms of white rot. **Soft rot**, also sometimes referred to as pocket rot, causes destruction of both cellulose and lignin. Soft rot can generally be found in isolated areas throughout the trunk and branch wood.

SAPWOOD ROT VS. HEARTWOOD ROT

Heartwood rot feeds upon the older dead xylem cells in the tree. **Heartwood rots** are responsible for the natural hollowing out of trees that have been wounded in the past. **Sapwood rot** affects the outer layers of wood and bark and is particularly destructive as it kills living tissues in the cambium and other essential tissues. Sapwood rot will generally display as many tiny fruiting bodies and can seriously weaken branches and stems. Heartwood rot includes most conk-forming fungi, but fruiting bodies do not have to be evident for heart rot to be present in a tree. Trees suffering from sapwood rot should be considered very dangerous and it is very important that climbers and other landscape professionals be able to identify this type of decay.

Tree Analysis

VISUAL INSPECTION

Arborists conducting a visual inspection of a tree should use a systematic approach that considers all parts of the tree in question. They should first look for evidence of **dieback**, or death of part of or the entire tree crown. This can be difficult with dormant trees in the winter, but experienced arborists will learn to distinguish living buds from dead ones. Next, the arborist will examine the **lean** of the tree and take note of any branches that seem overextended or likely to fail from excess weight. The taper of the tree trunk and branches should be gradual, and free of any wounds or fruiting bodies. Finally, the **root flare and base of the trunk** should be examined for signs of decay or defect. Damage in this area can indicate a potential for whole tree failure.

SOUNDING

Sounding is a relatively unsophisticated method for finding decay or hollow spots within a tree. A rubber mallet is used to strike the tree. Based on the quality of the sound, the arborist can get a general idea of how **hollow** the tree is. Practice is required to become proficient in this technique, but when mastered it can be an effective tool for quickly determining levels of decay in trees. It is important that the mallet be rubber or soft plastic to avoid damaging the bole of the tree.

DRILLING TECHNIQUES (DRILL/RESISTOGRAPH)

A resistograph is an advanced inspection tool that provides the arborist with a detailed readout of possible decay within the stem of a tree. The **restistograph** is paired with a **drill**, and when drilled into the tree, can record the amount of resistance encountered by the drill bit. A simpler version of this tool is called an **increment borer**. This is where just a standard drill is used, usually with some type of soft foam marker on the drill bit to indicate how deep the drill has penetrated. With practice, an increment borer can become an effective tool in determining tree decay. The downside of both of these methods is that they leave holes in the tree that are open wounds for further decay.

Trunk Flare/Root Excavation (Pneumatic Air Tools)

Air excavation is a means by which arborists can examine the buried parts of trees, including the root collar and lateral root system. High-pressure air is forced through a nozzle on an **air knife** and soil is blasted away, leaving the root system exposed. While damaging some of the fibrous root system, air excavation leaves a majority of the roots intact if preformed correctly. Air excavation is also a recommended method for mitigating the effects of highly compacted soil and can be used to perform techniques such as **radial trenching**. After conducting air excavation, native soil or lightly amended soil should be reapplied over the roots to prevent them from drying out and being killed.

New Technology

A **tomogram** is a device that measures the way sound travels through a tree trunk to determine the presence of internal decay. Sensors are places around the circumference of the tree and the tree is struck with a mallet to create an acoustic wave that is picked up by sensors and recorded. Other advanced methods include **X-ray systems** and **lateral pull tests** that measure how the tree responds to movement in its crown. Conducting these types of tests can be very expensive and are usually part of an advanced tree assessment program for high value landscape trees.

Risk Based on Tree Characteristic for Location

Fruit

The fruit produced by some trees can create unsafe conditions if planted near areas of **high traffic** or where large numbers of pedestrians walk. The coconut palm (Cocos nucifera) grows fruit that can exceed 3 pounds in weight and can injure or kill people and animals that happen to be underneath when they are shed. The female gingko tree (Gingko biloba), similarly produces large crops of fruit that are dropped during the fall and creates slip hazards on sidewalks. Other trees produce fruit that emits foul odors or attracts insects that feed on fallen fruit. Options to prevent these types of conflicts include **tree selection** (planting only male gingko trees) or **maintenance** (coconuts can be pruned from the tree on an annual basis). **Chemical applications** of compounds that prevent the creation of fruit are also an option for some species but must be applied annually.

Line of Sight Blockage

Tree shape and growth habits can sometimes create a hazard when planted in areas where human activity requires a **clear line of sight**. Wide, sprawling trees can create **visual obstructions** in places like traffic intersections, making it difficult for people to see pedestrians or cross traffic. Trees growing near roads can obscure signs and traffic lights, additionally creating hazards for drivers. If a tree must be planted near an intersection, consider using a species with a vase-shaped habit such as crepe myrtle (Lagerstroemia sp.) over a fastigiate (wide multi-stemmed tree) variety. Columnar, or tall and thin trees, may be a good option for the center areas of boulevards or along buildings that border streets.

Risk Mitigation

Prioritize

Applying a standardized system for determining **tree risk** will aid property owners in separating tree risks that require immediate attention from those that may only require monitoring. Various **risk management rating systems** exist, but proper **documentation** that takes into consideration the tree's growing site and history is the most important part of tree risk assessment. The more accurate the information available to the tree owner, the better they can consider their own risk tolerance and make decisions governing the management and mitigation of individual risk elements.

OPTIONS

Mitigation includes any practices meant to reduce the likelihood of tree failure. Generally, pruning is recommended to prevent structural failure and may be paired with support systems such as cables and braces. These systems should always be accompanied by a monitoring program.
Removal is recommended for trees where the risk level has attained unsatisfactory levels and mitigation efforts will not effectively remove the problem. Trees that are hollow or have heavy decay leave few options for arborists to remedy. Filling of hollows or wounds is no longer recommended and can have detrimental effects on tree health. Removal of decayed wood is also not an effective way to mitigate the effects of wood-destroying pathogens, and prevention of further decay by encouraging good tree health may be the only option for trees with decay.

Tree Support and Lightning Protection

Tree Support and Cabling

ANCHOR HARDWARE
ANSI A300 *Standards for Tree Support Systems* gives specifics on **cabling hardware** for use in tree support systems and should be consulted before determining what hardware will be needed for a specific tree application. **Eye-bolts** are commonly used to attach steel cable to a tree and full thickness holes must be pre-drilled before they are installed. Holes should be 1/16-1/8 inch larger than the hardware. **Amon-eye bolts** are similar but have a captive eye hole that is allowed to rotate on the bolt. Lag eyes are similar to eye bolts, but they screw into a hole with threading and do not pass all the way through the tree. **J-hooks** have a J-shaped attachment point rather than a ring and are also screwed into the tree by way of a small, pre-drilled hole.

THIMBLES AND BEND RADIUS
Dead-end grips are pre-made wire rope products that allow for easy termination of cable ends to anchor hardware. **Thimbles** are round metal sleeves designed to assist with the bend radius of the termination and make the system stronger. **Bend radius** is the size of the eye created when cable or rope passes around a circular object. Correctly sized thimbles should be used when affixing dead-end cables to J-hooks or other anchor hardware. Thimbles will also help reduce the wear on hardware as the tree moves in the wind.

CABLING TOOLS
Come-alongs are mechanical tools that use mechanical advantage to pull two objects together and are useful for tensioning cables prior to final attachment. A **cable grip** is generally used to grab the cable as it is tensioned with a come-along or similar device. **Cable aids** are tools that assist with twisting the wire ends of a dead-end grip around itself and can be used to pry open thimbles. **Ship auger bits** are used to drill holes in trees and are generally used with electric or gas-powered drills to create holes for eye-lags and amon-eye bolts. **Hacksaws and cable cutters** are useful for cutting steel rope or trimming excess threading off of bolts.

CABLE PLACEMENT
Cables should be placed roughly 2/3 the distance between the union of the two branches and the top of the crown. Cables should be installed in branches that are large enough to support the forces created by the branches and, if necessary, two or more cables can be used. The cable should be oriented perpendicular to the union of the two branches and, if multiple cables are installed, they should be separated by at least one branch diameter. Multiple cables should never be aligned vertically with each other and more than one cable should never be terminated on the same piece of anchor hardware.

DYNAMIC SUPPORT SYSTEMS
Dynamic cabling systems such as Cobra and TreeSave use **textile cordage** rather than wire rope to cable tree parts together. These materials are more flexible and stretch with the tree as it moves during windy conditions. Attachment points are created by wrapping the cordage around the tree through a webbing chafe sleeve to prevent friction against the bark. The ends are spliced back onto each other to form eyes that require no holes to be drilled in the tree. **Dynamic cables** are lighter and easier to install than steel rope systems, though their effectiveness is still being determined through testing.

BRACING

Tree braces usually consist of a threaded rod that is placed through a weakened or decayed crotch and are generally used alongside **cabling** to prevent tree failure. If a single rod is being placed in a tree, it will generally be situated two branch diameters above the crotch. If multiple braces are being employed, they should be placed below the union and offset by at least one branch diameter to prevent a weak column of decay from forming along the vertical axis. The ends of the threaded rod should be fitted with galvanized washers and nuts and the ends should be peened, or hit with a metal hammer, to prevent the nuts from unscrewing. The holes should be drilled 1/16-1/8 inch larger than the threaded rod to be installed and a drill bit that is long enough to pass through the entire tree should be used to bore the hole.

GUYING

Guying is used to support entire trees that may be structurally unsound by tethering them to the ground or another tree to prevent failure. The same hardware used for cabling systems is used for tree guys and anchors should be sufficiently strong to support the tree. Terminations should be located more than halfway up the tree to be supported, and on the bottom half of the anchor tree or to a sufficiently strong anchor point on the ground. If there is going to be pedestrian traffic near the guyed tree, the anchor end should be terminated at least 7 feet above the ground.

PROPPING

A tree that has a limb that is growing downwards towards the ground and is at risk to failure is a great candidate for a **tree prop**. Tree props are placed between the branch and the ground and provide structural support for horizontally growing tree parts. Props should not hinder the growth of the branch and should be securely anchored to the ground and branch to prevent them from falling away from the branch. A hole can be dug to assist with stabilizing the prop and it should be aligned vertically from the ground to prevent tipping. Props should be made of a rigid material such as steel rods or wood, oftentimes from branch material that has been pruned from the tree. Like all tree support systems, props should be inspected regularly.

Lightning Protection

TREES AND LIGHTNING

When lightning strikes trees, it causes internal damage from the heat and energy produced as energy travels down the trunk of the tree and into the ground. Sometimes **vertical wounds** are created as bark is blown off and internal damage can affect the ability of the tree to transport water or nutrients. Lightning strikes can also **kill** entire trees or act as openings for **insects or pathogens** to enter the tree. **Side flash** occurs when the electrical pathway jumps away from the tree to another tree or structure and can start fires or damage electrical systems located nearby. Side flash can also kill or severely injure people who are in close proximity to struck trees.

TREES BENEFITING FROM PROTECTION

Trees that are living in open areas or near bodies of water are more likely to be struck by lightning. Trees located on hilltops in areas where thunderstorms occur have a higher incidence of lightning damage, as lightning tends to strike the highest point in an area. As **lightning protection systems** are very expensive to install, generally only high-value trees or trees that are located in close proximity to structures are considered for protection. Tree species may play a part in the likelihood of being struck, though further research is necessary to confirm this theory.

Tree Protection Components

All tree lightning protection systems are composed of three basic components: air terminals, conductors, and ground terminals. **Air terminals** are the pieces of hardware located near the top of the tree where electrical flow from lightning is first introduced into the system. Air terminals are generally made of copper and are placed at the top of the tree and on major branch ends. **Conductors** are the copper wires that guide electricity downwards to the ground and are connected to the air terminals. Finally, **ground terminals** are the components that allow electricity flowing down the conductors to enter the earth. Ground terminals are composed of copper or steel rods or plates that are buried below the surface to ensure effective grounding.

Installation of Tree Protection Systems

Air terminals should be placed as high in the tree as practical and as far out on main branches as feasible. **Conductors** should travel in a straight line down branches and trunks towards the ground terminals and be free of kinks. **Ground terminals** have specific design criteria based on the type of terminal being used, the size of the system, and the soil type. Details of how to install ground terminals and other lightning protection componentry are located in **ANSI A300 *(Part 4) Lightning Protection Systems*** and this document should be consulted prior to installation of any lightning system. Inspection of lightning protection systems should be conducted routinely, and air terminals will have to be moved as the tree grows in height and branches grow longer.

Arborist Practice Test

1. Which of the following devices is used to prevent excessive wear to a cable that is attached to anchoring hardware?
   a. Cable aid
   b. Lag hook
   c. Ship auger
   d. Thimble

2. Which of the following is NOT an adverse consequence of lion tailing?
   a. Water sprouts
   b. Sunburned bark
   c. Barber chair
   d. Weak branches

3. If a branch is tip-tied, which section will fall away from the cut?
   a. Tip end
   b. Butt end
   c. Middle
   d. It is impossible to predict.

4. Mycorrhizae are the beneficial relationships between tree roots and
   a. grasses.
   b. fungi.
   c. insects.
   d. mulch.

5. In which of these pruning techniques does the arborist cut the branch back to a relatively weak point?
   a. Heading cut
   b. Undercut
   c. Reduction cut
   d. Topping

6. Which of the following tools should only be used for connectors that seldom need to be opened?
   a. Carabiners
   b. Clevises
   c. Shackles
   d. Screw links

7. What would be the bend ratio of a rigging system with blocks if the diameter of the pulley is three times the size of the diameter of the rope?
   a. 3:1
   b. 2:1
   c. 1:3
   d. 1:1

8. What is the primary purpose of wound dressing?
   a. Protect against disease
   b. Reduce decay
   c. Prevent insect infestation
   d. Improve appearance

9. Using ropes and other equipment to remove limbs or bring down entire trees is known as
   a. notching.
   b. landing.
   c. shock-loading.
   d. rigging.

10. At which of the following soil pH levels would iron be most available to plants?
   a. 5
   b. 6
   c. 7
   d. 8

11. For which of the following branches would propping be most appropriate?
   a. A small branch
   b. A large branch
   c. A large branch growing parallel to the ground
   d. A small branch growing perpendicular to the ground

12. Which of the following is an abiotic disorder?
   a. Girdling roots
   b. Vascular wilt disease
   c. Nematodes
   d. Mites

13. With respect to rope, one cycle for a rigging line is defined as
   a. one lift.
   b. one drop.
   c. a single use of the full rope line.
   d. one lift and one drop.

14. In general, how deep should the initial notch be when felling a tree?
   a. At least 6 inches
   b. At least one-half the diameter of the tree
   c. No more than 12 inches
   d. No more than one-third of the diameter of the tree

15. How far away should an uninvolved worker stand from a tree that is being felled?
   a. At least two tree lengths
   b. At least 20 feet
   c. At least one tree length
   d. At least 10 feet

16. Which type of bacteria is essential in the production of humus?
   a. Proteobacteria
   b. Actinomycetes
   c. Nitrospirae
   d. Aquificae

17. Where should the arborist stand when lifting a heavy object?
   a. As far away from the object as possible
   b. At least 1 foot away from the object
   c. Directly above the object
   d. As close to the object as possible

18. In the Plant Health Care model the most common goal is
   a. suppression.
   b. eradication.
   c. a mortality spiral.
   d. augmentation.

19. What state is soil in after all gravitational water has drained and the soil contains both available and unavailable water?
   a. Irrigation
   b. Field capacity
   c. Saturation
   d. Permanent wilting point

20. When installing a false crotch, which knot should be used to attach the block to the tree?
   a. Blake's hitch
   b. Tautline hitch
   c. Cow hitch
   d. Prusik hitch

21. In which of the following trees would it be appropriate to use a lag-threaded rod?
   a. Small tree
   b. Decayed tree
   c. Tree with soft wood
   d. Large tree

22. What is leaching?
   a. The removal of nutrients from a tree by insects
   b. The slow decline of a tree that has insufficient sunlight
   c. The improvement of root health after soil aeration
   d. The process in which water washes chemicals out of the soil

23. What is the maximum portion of the leaf-bearing crown that should be removed during pruning?
   a. 10 percent
   b. 25 percent
   c. 50 percent
   d. 75 percent

24. The highly fertile area surrounding growing roots is called the
   a. periderm.
   b. rhizosphere.
   c. macropore.
   d. substrate.

25. Which of the following is an advantage of the bare-root trees sold by nurseries?
   a. They are comparatively inexpensive.
   b. They are small.
   c. They are easy to transplant.
   d. All of these are advantages of bare-root trees.

26. In a rigging system, which of the following is usually the weakest component?
   a. Pulley
   b. Rigging line
   c. Block
   d. Carabiner

27. Which type of grip is specially designed to be used with extra-high-strength cable?
   a. Chicago grip
   b. Come-along
   c. Haven grip
   d. Anchor grip

28. What is the first step in training a young tree?
   a. Select a desired structure.
   b. Remove dead or damaged branches.
   c. Identify the lowest permanent branch.
   d. Select scaffold branches.

29. Insects that carry plant pathogens are referred to as
   a. vectors.
   b. nematodes.
   c. galls.
   d. herbivores.

30. What type of drill bit should be used when installing hardware in a tree?
   a. Dowel
   b. Threaded rod
   c. Ship auger
   d. Wood spade

31. Resistance to changes in pH is also known as
   a. infiltration rate.
   b. cation exchange capacity.
   c. buffering capacity.
   d. volatilization.

32. What is the name for a group within a species that has one trait in complete distinction to the other members of the species and naturally breeds to that trait?

   a. Forma
   b. Subspecies
   c. Cultivar
   d. Variety

33. The plant growth regulators that inhibit the work of cell-elongating hormones are called

   a. anti-gibberellins.
   b. sieve tube elements.
   c. photosynthates.
   d. macronutrients.

34. Which of the following metrics provides the most accurate indicator of soil fertility?

   a. Soil pH
   b. Cation exchange capacity
   c. Buffering capacity.
   d. Water-holding capacity

35. Which of the following risk assessment techniques provides the least information?

   a. Root collar excavation
   b. Visual tree assessment
   c. Decay testing
   d. Aerial canopy inspection

36. What does reference evapotranspiration measure?

   a. The usual amount of rainfall in a given location
   b. The typical water content of the foliage for a species
   c. The water supply in a particular location
   d. The expected amount of plant and soil water loss given location and existing vegetation

37. Xeriscaping is intended to protect the landscape against

   a. drought.
   b. frost.
   c. sunburn.
   d. flood.

38. The post that is attached to the tree and is wrapped in a load line is known as a

   a. tagline.
   b. bollard.
   c. kerf.
   d. block.

39. A tree is said to be a "barber chair" when

   a. it may be felled without the use of wedges.
   b. it has been topped repeatedly.
   c. it splits upward from a back cut.
   d. it requires guy wires for support.

40. In which direction should a chain saw operator move if he or she loses control of the tree while felling?
   a. 45 degrees to either side of a line opposite to the intended direction of fall
   b. In a line opposite to the intended direction of fall
   c. In a line perpendicular to the intended direction of fall
   d. Along the intended direction of the fall

41. On which side of a tree should workers stand while limbing or bucking?
   a. The right side of the tree
   b. The left side of the tree
   c. Uphill from the tree
   d. Downhill from the tree

42. Groups of different plants that need roughly the same amount of water are called
   a. hydrozones
   b. aquasets.
   c. drought zones.
   d. xeriscapes.

43. What is the goal of integrated pest management?
   a. To introduce species that prey on pests
   b. To promote insect populations
   c. To eradicate pests
   d. To maintain a tolerable level of pest damage

44. Which of the following cuts is used in topping?
   a. Thinning cut
   b. Reduction cut
   c. Heading cut
   d. Pruning cut

45. Which of the following is NOT a common part of a biological control strategy for pests?
   a. Poison
   b. Parasites
   c. Predators
   d. Pathogens

46. What is the name for a large, irregularly shaped area of dead tissue on a leaf?
   a. Dieback
   b. Leaf blotch
   c. Scorch
   d. Gummosis

47. What is the name of the technique used to keep nuts from backing off in a tree-bracing operation?
   a. Propping
   b. Peening
   c. Guying
   d. Dead-ending

48. Which of the following is not a standard part of the fertilizer analysis printed on the container?
   a. Potassium phosphate
   b. Soluble potash
   c. Phosphoric acid
   d. Total nitrogen

49. With respect to the pull of the cable, in which direction should hardware be installed?
   a. It does not matter.
   b. Diagonally
   c. Perpendicularly
   d. Along the same line

50. When should plants that bloom on the wood from the previous season be pruned?
   a. After the blooms are shed
   b. After the first frost of the autumn
   c. Just after they bloom
   d. Winter

51. During construction, how far should the tree protection zone extend from the trunk of a young tree?
   a. 1 foot for each inch of trunk diameter
   b. Two times the trunk diameter
   c. At least 3 feet
   d. 10 feet

52. Which of the following is the most common source of tree problems?
   a. Mites
   b. Adverse environmental conditions
   c. Insects
   d. Pathogens

53. Which of the foilowing is NOT necessarily part of a complete fertilizer?
   a. Nitrogen
   b. Potassium
   c. Calcium
   d. Phosphorus

54. Which of the following structures is commonly found when there are codominant stems?
   a. Branch protection zone
   b. Branch collar
   c. Branch bark ridge
   d. Included bark

55. Which type of fertilizer is recommended for newly planted trees?
   a. Complete fertilizer
   b. Liquid fertilizer
   c. Injection fertilizer
   d. Slow-release nitrogen fertilizer

56. The greenhouse effect is caused by excess amounts of ____ in the atmosphere.
   a. nitrogen
   b. carbon
   c. oxygen
   d. helium

57. Which pruning technique may be used to correct the problems created by topping?
   a. Crown restoration
   b. Crown thinning
   c. Crown reduction
   d. Crown cleaning

58. How should the back be positioned when moving a heavy object from the ground?
   a. The back should be hunched.
   b. The back should be held in a normal position.
   c. The back should be held straight.
   d. The back should be twisted.

59. In a soil profile, what is the top horizon?
   a. B
   b. O
   c. A
   d. C

60. What factor determines the height of the lowest permanent branch during structural pruning?
   a. Location of the tree
   b. Intended function of the tree
   c. Both location and function
   d. Neither location nor function

61. A close collection of many palm flowers is known as a(n)
   a. inflorescence.
   b. frond.
   c. monocot.
   d. petiole.

62. How does the working-load limit of a rope compare to its tensile strength?
   a. The working-load limit is lower than the tensile strength.
   b. The working-load limit is higher than the tensile strength.
   c. The working-load limit is the same as the tensile strength.
   d. The working-load limit is unrelated to the tensile strength.

63. A turgid leaf is
   a. dehydrated.
   b. fully hydrated.
   c. serrated.
   d. bipinnate.

64. Cytokinins are produced in the ____ but are crucial for the growth of the ____.
   a. shoots, roots
   b. roots, leaves
   c. roots, shoots
   d. shoots, trunk

65. The slow process through which a tree becomes accustomed to variations in its environment is called
   a. acclimation.
   b. aggregation.
   c. hardening off.
   d. selection.

66. What percentage of an ideal soil is made up of mineral solids?
   a. 10 percent
   b. 25 percent
   c. 45 percent
   d. 80 percent

67. Which of the following statements about tree growth is true?
   a. Most trees are decurrent at the beginning of their lives and become more decurrent over time.
   b. Most trees are excurrent at the beginning of their lives and become more decurrent over time.
   c. Most trees are never truly excurrent or decurrent.
   d. It is impossible to predict when a tree will be excurrent or decurrent.

68. What is one advantage of common-grade cable over extra-high-strength cable?
   a. Common-grade cable is more malleable than extra-high-strength cable.
   b. Common-grade cable is less expensive than extra-high-strength cable.
   c. Common-grade cable is longer than extra-high-strength cable.
   d. Common-grade cable is more durable than extra-high-strength cable.

69. Why should thimbles be used when attaching a cable to anchoring hardware?
   a. To increase the abrasion on the cable
   b. To increase the bend radius of the cable
   c. To eliminate the need for eye splices
   d. To enable the use of extra-high-strength cable

70. Monocotyledons and dicotyledons are the two classes of
   a. arboriculture.
   b. morphology.
   c. gymnosperm.
   d. angiosperms.

71. When multiple cables are installed on the same limb, how much vertical space should there be between the sets of hardware?
   a. At least 3 feet
   b. The diameter of the base of the tree
   c. A minimum of one branch diameter's vertical space
   d. A maximum of 3 feet

72. What is the name for the base of the leaf stem, before the beginning of the blade?
   a. Petiole
   b. Midrib
   c. Petiolule
   d. Leaflet

73. What is the recommended minimum bend ratio for a pulley used as part of a block system in rigging?
   a. 1:1
   b. 2:1
   c. 3:1
   d. 4:1

74. What material is recommended for the connecting links used in rigging?
   a. Steel
   b. Titanium
   c. Aluminum
   d. Carbon alloy

75. What is the maximum number of cables that should be installed on a single eye bolt or lag?
   a. One
   b. Two
   c. Three
   d. There is no limit to the number of cables that may be installed on a single eye bolt or lag.

76. Which type of nursery stock has up to 90 percent of its absorbing roots removed before sale?
   a. Bare root
   b. Containerized
   c. Container grown
   d. Balled and burlapped

77. According to Alex Shigo's model, which wall is not part of the reaction zone?
   a. Wall 1
   b. Wall 2
   c. Wall 3
   d. Wall 4

78. What is the typical means of attaching common, seven-strand cable to hardware?
   a. Dead-end grips
   b. Cable stops
   c. Metal swages
   d. Eye splice

79. In which of the following are the classification terms listed from general to specific?
   a. Genus, family, order, class
   b. Order, class, phylum, kingdom
   c. Class, order, family, genus
   d. Family, class, order, genus

80. Hardiness is the tree's ability to withstand extremely ___ temperatures.
   a. moderate
   b. temperate
   c. hot or cold
   d. variable

81. In arboriculture, a witch's broom is
   a. a branch that has foliage only at its very end.
   b. a collection of spindly roots.
   c. a pattern of leaf spots.
   d. a cluster of weak secondary shoots.

82. When installing hardware in a tree, about how much larger in diameter should the drilled hole be than the hardware?
   a. one-sixteenth inch
   b. one-eighth inch
   c. one-fourth inch
   d. one-half inch

83. Which of the following is another name for the outermost rings of the xylem?
   a. Phloem
   b. Sapwood
   c. Cambium
   d. Heartwood

84. A tree that leans toward an area of sunlight is displaying a(n)
   a. phytotoxicity.
   b. trait.
   c. phototropism.
   d. assimilation.

85. Which of the following types of organic mulch will break down most slowly?
   a. Leaves
   b. Bark
   c. Lawn clippings
   d. Straw

86. When removing a dead branch, where should the final cut be made?
   a. Just outside the collar of living tissue
   b. A foot outside the collar of living tissue
   c. Just inside the collar of living tissue
   d. A foot inside the collar of living tissue

87. Which of the following is NOT a part of nutrient cycling?
   a. Organic material decomposes and nutrients are released into the soil.
   b. Trees die and their bodies disintegrate in the soil.
   c. Tree roots absorb nutrients from the soil.
   d. The nutrients in the soil are drawn into the atmosphere through transpiration.

88. Which of the following is a hybrid?
   a. *Nepenthes* × *hookeriana*
   b. *Acer saccharum*
   c. *Cornus florida* f. *rubra*
   d. *Gleditsia triacanthos* var. *inermis*

89. Why does pest resurgence occur?
   a. Environmental conditions encourage a sharp increase in the pest population.
   b. Indiscriminate pesticide use kills pests and their predators, but when the pesticides cease to be used the predators take longer to respond than the pests.
   c. The pest adapts to the particular pesticide being used.
   d. The arborist does not use enough pesticide.

90. Which watering strategy would an arborist use to encourage the development of deep roots?
   a. Infrequent and shallow
   b. Infrequent and deep
   c. Frequent and shallow
   d. Frequent and deep

91. Removing all of the lateral branches from a felled tree is called
   a. pruning.
   b. bucking.
   c. trimming.
   d. limbing.

92. When two trees are guyed together, where should the guys be installed?
   a. The guy on the supported tree should be above the midpoint, and the guy on the anchor tree should be on the lower half of the trunk.
   b. The guy on the supported tree should be above the midpoint, and the guy on the anchor tree should be on the upper half of the trunk.
   c. The guy on the supported tree should be below the midpoint, and the guy on the anchor tree should be on the lower half of the trunk.
   d. The guy on the supported tree should be below the midpoint, and the guy on the anchor tree should be on the upper half of the trunk.

93. What is the name for a small aperture in the bark, through which gases may travel?
   a. Follicle
   b. Ventricle
   c. Cuticle
   d. Lenticel

94. Which of the following colors would NOT be the product of a carotenoid pigment?
   a. Yellow
   b. Purple
   c. Red
   d. Orange

95. Which of the following trees is ring porous?
   a. Magnolia
   b. Birch
   c. Elm
   d. Beech

96. At the base of a branch, in which direction is the branch xylem oriented?
   a. Clockwise around the trunk
   b. Counterclockwise around the trunk
   c. Upward
   d. Downward

97. On which type of tree is brown rot most likely to be found?
   a. Conifer
   b. Palm
   c. Deciduous
   d. Fallen

98. What should be the minimum distance between two workers using chain saws at the same time on the same tree?
   a. 5 feet
   b. 10 feet
   c. 20 feet
   d. 50 feet

99. Which of the following factors does NOT affect the extent of damage when lightning strikes a tree?
   a. Moisture content
   b. Leaf thickness
   c. Wood porosity
   d. Bark thickness

100. As part of prescription fertilization, an arborist needs to obtain samples from
   a. the soil.
   b. the leaves.
   c. the soil and leaves
   d. neither the soil nor the leaves

101. Why do the side plates of an arborist block extend beyond the sheaves?
   a. To protect the hands of the arborist
   b. To keep the line from slipping
   c. To prevent abrasion of the line
   d. To encourage smooth passage of the line

102. When looking at a cross section of a branch, which ring represents the most recent year of growth?
   a. The first ring inside the cambium
   b. The first ring inside the phloem
   c. The first ring outside the cambium
   d. The first ring outside the phloem

103. When an arborist is cutting a branch with the top of the chain saw bar, how will the saw tend to behave?
   a. It will pull away from the arborist.
   b. It will move downhill.
   c. It will behave unpredictably.
   d. It will push back toward the arborist.

104. Which of the following can be used in place of a large screw link?
   a. Shackle
   b. Clevis
   c. Either a shackle or a clevis
   d. Neither a shackle or a clevis

105. As water and/or nutrient availability improves, the growth rate ___ and the allelochemical concentration ___.
   a. increases, decreases
   b. decreases, increases
   c. increases, increases
   d. decreases, decreases

106. In legal circumstances, a naturally occurring event that could not have been foreseen or prevented is called a(n)
   a. act of interest.
   b. inevitable act.
   c. liable act.
   d. act of God.

107. A nonindigenous species that will propagate without assistance and has become established in a particular area is classified as
   a. introduced.
   b. naturalized.
   c. invasive.
   d. native.

108. What is the name of the process by which bare-root nursery stock is rapidly changed from dormancy to growth?
   a. Sweating
   b. Heating
   c. Springing
   d. Hardening

109. In which notch commonly used in felling do the two cuts form an approximate right angle?
   a. Conventional notch
   b. Close-face notch
   c. Humboldt notch
   d. Open-face notch

110. When should a dormant horticultural oil be applied?
   a. Before bud break
   b. Midwinter
   c. Just after bud break
   d. Late summer

111. Which type of cable is often used for cabling trees?
   a. Extra-high-strength cable
   b. Common-grade, seven-strand, galvanized cable
   c. Both extra-high-strength cable and common-grade, seven-strand, galvanized cable
   d. Neither extra-high-strength cable nor common-grade, seven-strand, galvanized cable

112. Why does compost need to be turned and watered occasionally?
   a. To stifle microorganisms
   b. To maintain sufficient levels of oxygen and water
   c. To improve pH
   d. To discourage insect infestation

113. The open spaces in plant tissues are called
   a. symplasm.
   b. apoplasm.
   c. protoplasm.
   d. xenoplasm.

114. Which of the following is NOT a good reason for installing cables?
   a. They can support branches that hang over traffic areas.
   b. They can support codominant branches with included bark.
   c. They can help support decayed branches.
   d. They can counterbalance a weak root system.

115. The temporary housing of carbon dioxide in the wood and other tissues of a tree is known as

 a. carbon sequestration.
 b. carbon stabilization.
 c. carbon retention.
 d. carbon collection.

116. What is the name for the interaction between changes in weather and recurring biological phenomena?

 a. Morphology
 b. Phenology
 c. Tomography
 d. Hydrology

117. In which of the following does the rope not cross over itself?

 a. Bight
 b. Loop
 c. Turn
 d. Round turn

118. Why is the E horizon generally a lighter color than the A horizon?

 a. The E horizon is primarily composed of silt.
 b. The A horizon is primarily composed of sand.
 c. The A horizon has less organic material.
 d. The E horizon has less organic material.

119. With regard to rope, what is glazing?

 a. Melted fiber
 b. Stretched fiber
 c. Torn fiber
 d. Worn fiber

120. Plants that are specially adapted to dry conditions are called

 a. halophytes.
 b. hydrophytes.
 c. mesophytes.
 d. xerophytes.

121. An imbalance in which substance can lead to the harmful phenomenon of reverse osmosis?

 a. Nitrogen
 b. Oxygen
 c. Salt
 d. Water

122. A broad planting of the same species over a wide area is known as a
   a. monoculture.
   b. permaculture.
   c. monocot.
   d. pathogen.

123. Approximately how long should the hinge be when felling a tree?
   a. 80 percent of the diameter of the tree
   b. 25 percent of the diameter of the tree
   c. 25 percent of the height of the tree
   d. 10 percent of the height of the tree

124. Which of the following is NOT an advantage of using blocks instead of running lines through tree crotches?
   a. Blocks decrease the wear on the rigging lines.
   b. Blocks create a naturally uneven load on the rope.
   c. Blocks limit the damage to the tree.
   d. Blocks decrease the amount of force required to move an object.

125. Which of the following types of rope always has a cover and a core?
   a. three-strand rope
   b. 12-strand rope
   c. Kernmantle
   d. All of these always have a cover and a core.

126. In which macronutrient is a tree most likely to be deficient?
   a. Sulfur
   b. Phosphorus
   c. Potassium
   d. Nitrogen

127. Which of the following is NOT a common disease caused by bacteria?
   a. Heart rot
   b. Fire blight
   c. Crown gall
   d. Bacterial leaf scorch

128. Which of the following is a disadvantage of surface application of fertilizers to trees?
   a. Surface application takes more time than other methods of fertilization.
   b. Surface application requires complicated and expensive equipment.
   c. After surface application, fertilizer sometimes runs off into nearby bodies of water.
   d. Surface application delivers fertilizer to the parts of the tree that need it least.

129. A tree that displays early fall color most likely has problems with its
   a. crown.
   b. roots.
   c. scaffold branches.
   d. trunk.

130. In what type of climate is powdery mildew disease most prevalent?
   a. Cool and wet
   b. Cool and dry
   c. Warm and wet
   d. Warm and dry

131. Which of the following is a common cause of chronic stress?
   a. Poor drainage
   b. Early frost
   c. Lightning
   d. Fire

132. Which of the following trees should not be treated with fertilizer implants or injections?
   a. A tree that has never been treated in this manner before
   b. A tree that has been living in drought conditions
   c. A tree suffering from a micronutrient deficiency
   d. A tree that has not responded to traditional fertilizer application methods

133. How will the wetting pattern of a clay loam be different than that of a sandy loam?
   a. The clay loam will have a broader wetting pattern.
   b. The sandy loam will have a broader wetting pattern.
   c. The difference between the wetting patterns is unpredictable.
   d. There is no difference between the wetting pattern of a clay loam and the wetting pattern of a sandy loam.

134. What is the generally agreed-upon working-load limit for a new rope used for tree maintenance?
   a. 10 percent of the tensile strength
   b. 50 percent of the tensile strength
   c. 75 percent of the tensile strength
   d. 100 percent of the tensile strength

135. Which type of mold is based on the liquid waste of mealybugs?
   a. Dusty mold
   b. Black mold
   c. Sooty mold
   d. White mold

136. When climbing along the end of a horizontal branch, where should the arborist keep his or her weight?
   a. On the rope
   b. On the branch
   c. Centered
   d. On the trunk

137. The chemicals that have an adverse effect on some herbivores and pathogens are known as
   a. anti-gibberellins.
   b. actinomycetes.
   c. auxin.
   d. allelochemicals.

138. Which of the following is NOT one of the prerequisites for a claim of negligence?
   a. Personal injury
   b. Breach of duty
   c. Harm
   d. Duty

139. What is the name for the part of a rope that is not in use?
   a. Lead
   b. Working end
   c. Fall
   d. Running end

140. In plant care, what is the difference between vitality and vigor?
   a. Vigor is associated with unusually large growth, while vitality has more to do with survival.
   b. Vigor is the plant's genetic ability to handle stress, while vitality is its ability to thrive in a particular environment.
   c. Vitality depends on proper care, while vigor is a natural condition.
   d. There is no difference between vitality and vigor.

141. What is the formula for counting degree days?
   a. Divide the threshold value by the daily average temperature
   b. Divide the daily average temperature by the threshold value
   c. Subtract the threshold value from the daily average temperature
   d. Subtract the daily average temperature from the threshold value

142. Which part of the tree produces most of the auxin?
   a. Shoot tips
   b. Roots
   c. Xylem
   d. Heartwood

143. The edge of the tree crown is also known as the
   a. crown edge.
   b. foliage dome.
   c. drip line.
   d. ring zone.

144. With use, the working-load limit of a rope will
   a. increase.
   b. decrease.
   c. stay the same.
   d. change unpredictably.

145. Why should metal washers be used when installing cables with eye bolts or threaded rods?
   a. To prevent the bolt from being damaged
   b. To eliminate decay from the installation site
   c. To keep the nut from being pulled through the tree
   d. To reduce pest infestations

146. How does the load on a piece of rope relate to the weight of the object creating the load?
   a. The load may change, but the weight stays the same.
   b. The load stays the same, but the weight may change.
   c. Neither the load nor the weight may change.
   d. Both the load and the weight may change.

147. To avoid salt burn, fertilizers should have a salt index below
   a. 10
   b. 30
   c. 50
   d. 100

148. How does Dutch elm disease spread?
   a. Fungi
   b. Insects
   c. Wind
   d. Root graft

149. Which of the following phenomena does NOT indicate problems with a leaning tree?
   a. Soil cracks
   b. Raised roots
   c. Reaction wood
   d. Mounded soil

150. A positively charged ion is called a(n)
   a. electron.
   b. cation.
   c. anion.
   d. proton.

151. Which of the following tree cabling configurations is the most complex?
   a. Hub and spoke
   b. Box
   c. Rotary
   d. Triangular

152. Which section of roots exhibits the most aggressive growth?
   a. Sinker roots
   b. The roots near the surface
   c. The lateral roots deep beneath the surface
   d. Root crown

153. When is the best time to apply a micronutrient spray to trees?
   a. Just before a period of heavy growth
   b. At the beginning of winter
   c. At dusk
   d. Immediately after transplantation

154. Which of these factors would affect the microclimate of a location?
   a. Topography
   b. Average rainfall
   c. Soil profile
   d. All of the above

155. Which of the following is a typical concentration for slow-release supplemental nitrogen fertilizers used under normal conditions?
   a. 4 pounds of nitrogen per thousand square feet of root area
   b. 40 pounds of nitrogen per thousand square feet of root area
   c. 10 pounds of nitrogen per thousand square feet of root area
   d. 100 pounds of nitrogen per thousand square feet of root area

156. Which of the following knots is primarily used for sending equipment up to a climber?
   a. Running bowline
   b. Midline clove hitch
   c. Figure-eight knot
   d. Endline clove hitch

157. What is the typical treatment for highly sodic soil?
   a. Application of slow-release fertilizer with low nitrogen content
   b. Application of slow-release fertilizer with high nitrogen content
   c. Irrigation with high-sodium water
   d. Irrigation with low-sodium water

158. What are codominant stems?
   a. Two stems that feed from the same root
   b. Two stems that intertwine
   c. Two stems that are much larger than all of the other stems that grow from the same place
   d. Two stems with roughly equal size that grow from the same place

159. Which of the following methods of starting a chain saw is NOT recommended?
   a. On the ground
   b. Leglock method
   c. Drop starting
   d. All of these methods are recommended.

160. Which of the following components is NOT part of a lightning protection system?
   a. Air terminal
   b. Ground terminal
   c. Conductors
   d. Battery

161. In the CTLA trunk formula method, what is the primary determinant of a tree's value?
   a. Location
   b. Health
   c. Size
   d. Foliage

162. When applying fertilizer with the drill-hole method, how far away from the trunk should the concentric rings of holes extend?
   a. At least to the drip line
   b. No farther than the drip line
   c. 1 foot from the root crown
   d. 5 feet from the root crown

163. What is the appropriate minimum diameter for a main branch used for tying in?
   a. 2 inches
   b. 4 inches
   c. 6 inches
   d. 8 inches

164. What is the difference between an open and a closed throwing knot?
   a. A closed throwing knot should not be tied with kernmantle rope.
   b. An open throwing knot is more likely to get caught in branches.
   c. A closed throwing knot requires the use of hardware.
   d. An open throwing knot will come undone when the rope is thrown.

165. In structural pruning, the process of reducing competing stems into laterals is known as
   a. subordination.
   b. hardening off.
   c. heading.
   d. raising.

166. What is deficient in a leaf that displays chlorosis?
   a. Glucose
   b. Chlorophyll
   c. Vitamin D
   d. Water

167. When planting a large tree, why is it a bad idea to fill the bottom of the hole with gravel?
   a. Soil is likely to slip down into the gravel, leaving a crater around the tree trunk.
   b. Gravel can leach harmful chemicals into the soil.
   c. The soil can become excessively saturated.
   d. Gravel is inhospitable to beneficial organisms in the soil.

168. What is another name for irregular plant growth, often found in the leaf tissue?
   a. Blotch
   b. Scorch
   c. Spot
   d. Galls

169. In which arrangement are the leaflets of a compound leaf placed along a single stem, but with a petiolule for each leaflet?
   a. Bipalmate
   b. Bipinnate
   c. Pinnate
   d. Palmate

170. What is the difference between simple and compound leaves?
   a. A simple leaf does not have serrations.
   b. A simple leaf is round while a compound leaf has an oblong shape.
   c. A simple leaf has a single midrib while a compound leaf has two.
   d. A simple leaf has a single leaf blade while a compound leaf may have several leaflets.

171. Which of the following is a synthetic organic fertilizer?
   a. Peat
   b. Urea formaldehyde
   c. Fish hydrolysates
   d. Bloodmeal

172. What is the name for a variety that must be grown by humans and that needs human attention to perpetuate a particular trait?
   a. Variety
   b. Forma
   c. Subspecies
   d. Cultivar

173. For which of the following tasks would a loose-weave, hollow-braid, polyester 12-strand rope be appropriate?
   a. Rigging slings
   b. Climbing
   c. Rigging
   d. This rope would not be appropriate for any of these tasks.

174. Maple, ash, dogwood, and horse chestnut are the main genera of trees that have a(n) ____ leaf arrangement.
   a. alternate
   b. opposite
   c. whorled
   d. undulate

175. What number of needles is NOT commonly found in a pine fascicle sheath?
   a. Two
   b. Three
   c. Four
   d. Five

176. What is the most popular climbing hitch for climbers in the United States?
   a. Blake's hitch
   b. Tautline hitch
   c. Midline clove hitch
   d. Endline clove hitch

177. Why is lignin important to tree health?
   a. Lignin makes wood resistant to compression.
   b. Lignin transports nutrients through the tree.
   c. Lignin helps the tree survive cold weather.
   d. Lignin improves the ability of leaves to perform transpiration.

178. How is the working-load limit of a rope calculated?
   a. Tensile strength multiplied by design factor
   b. Cycles to failure multiplied by design factor
   c. Tensile strength divided by cycles to failure
   d. Tensile strength divided by design factor

179. Why is it valuable for a stem to have good taper?
   a. A stem with good taper is able to produce more fruit.
   b. A stem with good taper is less likely to break when subjected to a force.
   c. A stem with good taper is better able to absorb nutrients.
   d. A stem with good taper is a sturdy perch for insects.

180. In a command-and-response system, when should the climber move up the tree?
   a. After his or her assistant knocks on the tree trunk three times
   b. After five seconds
   c. After he or she has heard an acknowledgement
   d. After he or she has indicated his or her plans

181. Which of the following is NOT one of the characteristics of a pest, as defined in the integrated pest management system?
   a. Requires intervention
   b. Competes with good plants for resources
   c. Decreases the appearance of the landscape
   d. Decreases the safety of the landscape

182. When is it appropriate to use climbing spurs?
   a. When the tree is going to be removed
   b. When the tree is decayed
   c. When the tree has an especially broad crown
   d. When the tree is a conifer

183. What is the name of the radial planes of living cells that extend through the phloem and xylem?
   a. Heartwood
   b. Rays
   c. Vessels
   d. Cambium

184. In most living trees, which of the following is dead?

a. Sapwood
b. Cambium
c. Heartwood
d. Xylem

185. If a tree has an especially large diameter, how should the hinge be adjusted?

a. It should be smaller.
b. It should be larger.
c. It should be deeper.
d. It does not need to be adjusted.

186. On a chain saw, the upper part of the guide bar tip is also known as the

a. patrol section.
b. safety segment.
c. kickback quadrant.
d. applicator tip.

187. What determines the type of damage done by an insect to a tree?

a. The prevalence of predators
b. The insect's mouthparts
c. The species of tree
d. the thickness of the bark

188. In the ANSI standards, what word indicates a recommendation?

a. *Must*
b. *Could*
c. *Shall*
d. *Should*

189. What is the optimal level of pore space in a soil?

a. 25 percent
b. 50 percent
c. 75 percent
d. 100 percent

190. Which type of knot would be recommended for binding two ropes with different diameters?

a. Prusik hitch
b. Double fisherman's knot
c. Sheet bend
d. Cow hitch with half hitch

191. Which type of nursery stock is least susceptible to girdling roots upon planting?

a. Balled and burlapped
b. Bare root
c. Containerized
d. Container grown

192. What is the minimum tensile strength for the snaps and carabiners used in climbing?
   a. 500 pounds
   b. 1000 pounds
   c. 5000 pounds
   d. 10,000 pounds

193. What color are most new roots?
   a. White
   b. Red
   c. Brown
   d. Black

194. When a tree has substantial decay on one side, where should the back cut be finished?
   a. Below the decay
   b. Above the decay
   c. On the undecayed side of the tree
   d. On the decayed side of the tree

195. What does the acronym CODIT stand for?
   a. Cover Of Damage In Trees
   b. Compartmentalization Of Decay In Trees
   c. Containment Of Detritus In Trees
   d. Core Of Disease In Trees

196. In a small tree, approximately how much vertical space should there be between scaffold branches?
   a. 6 inches
   b. 1 foot
   c. 2 feet
   d. 3 feet

197. What is the name for the bud at the end of a twig?
   a. Axillary bud
   b. Node
   c. Lateral bud
   d. Terminal bud

198. A tensiometer measures
   a. air pressure.
   b. soil moisture.
   c. root length.
   d. nutrient availability.

199. The process through which leaves lose water vapor is called
   a. condensation.
   b. aspiration.
   c. transpiration.
   d. exhalation.

200. Frass is a combination of insect waste and
   a. sawdust.
   b. sap.
   c. pollen.
   d. soil.

Answer Key and Explanations

1. D: A thimble is used to prevent excessive wear to a cable that is attached to anchoring hardware. The thimble can also be used to protect the termination loop of the cable, or, when it is used with rope, to increase the bend radius. A cable aid is a tool used to tighten lag screws, open steel thimbles, and wrap dead-end grips. A lag hook, otherwise known as a J-hook, is a lag-threaded cable anchor that has an open eye. A ship auger is a type of drill bit that is shaped like an open spiral. Arborists use these types of bits when drilling holes for bracing or cable installation.

2. C: Barber chair is not an adverse consequence of lion tailing. However, lion tailing may lead to water sprouts, sunburned bark, or weak branches. A water sprout is a shoot that grows epicormically from latent buds on the trunk or branches. Sunburn is caused by heat damage on thin or juvenile bark that has been exposed to direct sun rays. When inner branches of trees are excessively pruned the upper side of branches can be newly exposed to sunlight causing sunburn. Lions tailing can also cause branches to develop with poor taper and make them more likely to fail from structural weakness.

3. B: If a branch is tip-tied, the butt end will fall away from the cut. Tip-tying is the technique of tying a line at the tip end of the limb that is to be removed. The extent to which the branch will swing out is largely dependent on where the rigging point is positioned. Climbers should be careful when tip-tying to avoid the path through which the swinging limb is likely to fall. In some cases, the arborist will tip-tie the branch and have a ground person lift it off the cut with mechanical advantage so that it will not impact a target located below the climber.

4. B: Mycorrhizae are the beneficial relationships between tree roots and fungi. This sort of mutually advantageous relationship is called symbiosis. Mycorrhizae may be either ectotrophic or endotrophic, depending on whether the fungus lives inside or outside the root, respectively. Mycorrhizae are important for trees because they increase the area through which minerals (especially phosphorus) may be absorbed. Fungi benefit by absorbing carbohydrates from the plant tissues.

5. A: In a heading cut, the arborist cuts the branch back to a relatively weak point. A heading cut, also known as heading back the branch, is the process of cutting the shoot for the branch back to the buds, stubs, or the closest lateral branch that cannot assume dominance. A heading cut may also be made on older trees where avoiding a large wound on the trunk may be an objective. A reduction cut is a pruning technique that takes the branch or stem back to a lateral branch that is big enough to be apically dominant. Topping is the practice of cutting a tree back to stubs, internodes, buds, or lateral branches that are not great enough to assume apical dominance.

6. D: Screw links should only be used for connectors that seldom need to be opened. A carabiner is an oblong metal ring that opens or closes with a spring-loaded gate. Carabiners can be used in both dynamic and static rigging. A clevis is a fitting that is shaped like a U and has a pin running through it. A screw link is a connecting device that has a threaded closure mechanism. It is used to quickly attach branches to rigging lines or various climbing and rigging componentry together.

7. A: If the diameter of the pulley is three times the size of the diameter of the rope, the bend ratio of the rigging system with blocks is 3:1. The bend ratio is the relationship between the diameter of a branch or sheave to the diameter of the rope wrapped around it. It is important for the bend ratio of a rigging system with blocks to be at least 4:1, because an excessively large rope for a given pulley can lead to rope and block damage.

8. D: The primary purpose of wound dressing is to improve appearance. Formerly, wound dressings were used to prevent decay and the introduction of diseases, but many of these claims have been found to be unsubstantiated. Some evidence shows that using certain wound coverings may help prevent the detection of wounds by opportunistic insects that spread oak wilt, but further research is necessary to support these claims. For this reason, wound dressings are only rarely used at present and almost entirely to improve the appearance of the tree. When an arborist does elect to use a dressing, he or she should ensure that the substance will not damage the tree and that it is applied lightly.

9. D: Using ropes and other equipment to remove limbs or bring down entire trees is known as rigging. Notching is cutting a wedge into tree trunk or branch before preforming a back cut to complete the cut. Landing is the lowering of branches to the ground. Arborists should establish a landing zone near the tree. This will be the area where large branches and foliage are to land during removal. Shock-loading is the sudden application of a dynamic force on the rope or rigging equipment when a moving load is stopped abruptly.

10. A: Of the given soil pH levels, iron would be most available in soil with a pH of 5. The optimal pH range for absorption varies for different elements. However, all of the major elements are available in sufficient amounts when the soil pH is between 6 and 7.5. For soil, the essential elements are nitrogen, phosphorus, potassium, sulfur, calcium, magnesium, iron, manganese, boron, copper, zinc, and molybdenum. Elements are defined as essential when they are required for the tree's development or metabolism.

11. C: Propping would be most appropriate for a large branch growing parallel to the ground. Propping, as the name suggests, is the interposition of solid structures between a branch and the ground. This technique is used when it is not practicable or desired to remove a branch, but there is concern about it falling down onto an object or the ground. There is no set rule for prop material: wood, metal, and concrete have all been used to create effective props. The arborist simply needs to ensure that the chosen material will be strong enough to handle the branch and that there will be sufficient maintenance of the prop once it is in place. Also, the prop should in no way restrict the subsequent growth of the branch. The top of the prop should have some kind of divot or scoop that holds the branch in place without restricting its growth. Usually, the support for the prop will be solidified by burying it in the ground, though care should be taken to ensure that the roots are not damaged.

12. A: Girdling roots are an abiotic disorder. The term *abiotic* means nonliving. Girdling roots are caused by roots that grow around each other causing constriction. One common sign of girdling roots is weak vegetative growth on the lateral branches along one side of the tree. Vascular wilt disease causes a discoloration of the xylem. A vascular wilt disease interferes with the transport of water and nutrients, eventually leading to the tree's death. Nematodes are tiny roundworms, some of which feed on plant tissues. Mites are arachnids sometimes live and feed on plant parts. Mites may cause galls on plants to create reproductive structures or may suck the fluids from the leaves and stems.

13. D: With respect to rope, one cycle for a rigging line is defined as one lift and one drop. The amount of wear on a rigging line is measured in cycles. Specifically, the longevity of a rope can be measured in cycles to failure. No matter how well the rope is maintained, each cycle of use damages it. A rope that is treated poorly or is dirty will age even faster. A rope may fail long before it reaches its cycles-to-failure mark.

14. D: In general, the initial notch when felling a tree should be no more than one-third of the diameter of the tree. The length of the hinge, on the other hand, should be about four-fifths of the tree's diameter. The basic approach to felling a tree is a notch followed by a back cut. Arborists will use conventional notches, Humboldt notches, and open-face notches. A larger notch gives the arborist a longer period of control over the tree. The arborist should try to avoid placing the notches anywhere around decay or cracks, because solid fiber makes for a much better hinge. Also, the arborist should avoid bypassing the notch apex during the cuts, because bypassing cuts may break the most important fibers for controlling the hinge.

15. A: An uninvolved worker should stand at least two tree lengths from a tree that is being felled. A worker who is involved in the process should be at least one tree length away and should have an escape path. Involved workers should also be sure that they have an effective means of communicating with the worker at the base of the tree. Every worker on the scene should understand his or her role and responsibilities.

16. B: Actinomycetes are essential in the production of humus. These bacteria increase the buffering capacity of the soil and encourage decomposition, which is essential for the creation of humus. Humus is the compost part of soil, made up of decomposed and partially decomposed organic material.

17. D: When lifting a heavy object, the arborist should stand as close to the object as possible. Arborists are often called upon to lift heavy objects, so they should know the proper technique. To begin with, the arborist should check the path along which the object will move, to ensure that it is free of obstacles and hazards. The arborist should survey the object, looking for sharp edges or splinters. The intention during the survey is to find the best way to grip the object. It is never a bad idea to perform a brief trial lift, just to make sure that completing the task will be possible. The arborist should set his or her feet shoulder-width apart and establish a solid center of gravity. Then, when it is time to lift the object, the arborist should crouch as near the load as possible, bending his or her legs. Contrary to conventional wisdom, it is not necessarily optimal to keep the back totally straight when lifting a heavy object. Instead, the arborist should maintain his or her normal posture, so long as it is reasonably correct. It is important for most of the work to be done by the legs rather than the back.

18. A: In the Plan Health Care pest control model the most common goal is suppression. In other words, the intention is to diminish but not entirely eradicate pests. Arborists typically opt for a suppression strategy because it requires fewer pesticides and does not subject the tree to severe shocks. Eradication is really only an option when dealing with the most aggressive and dangerous pests. When possible, plant health care practitioners try to prevent pest infestation and plant damage before other interventions are necessary.

19. B: Field capacity of a soil has been reached when all of the gravitational or macropore occupying water has drained from the soil leaving available and unavailable water. The remaining water is held in the micropores of the soil and is sometimes known as capillary water. This water is available to the plant to uptake through its fibrous root structure. Irrigation is the process of applying water to soil. Saturation refers the point where water can no longer be absorbed by the soil and begins to run off. Permanent wilting point refers to a state of foliage desiccation whereby the leaves of a plant have become so dehydrated that they cannot return to normal function and die.

20. C: When installing a false crotch, the block should be attached to the tree with a cow hitch. After the knot has been tied, the arborist should add two half hitches near the splice, adjacent to the bight in the cow hitch. A cow hitch is tied by leading the working end of the sling around the stem, beneath the splice, and around again in the opposite direction. A Blake's hitch is a common climbing knot along with the tautline hitch, both utilized to advance and descend a climbing line. A prussic hitch is a generic term for any friction hitch, but sometimes refers to a girth hitch or English prussic knot specifically.

21. A: It would be appropriate to use a lag-threaded rod in a small tree. Lag-threaded rods should not be used in decayed trees, large trees, or trees with soft wood. For these trees, only machine-threaded rods will do. The difference between the two types of rod is that the lag-threaded rod has fewer threads per inch of rod and is self-anchoring. When machine-threaded rods are used, the drilled hole should be one-sixteenth to one-eighth inch larger in diameter than the rod.

22. D: Leaching is the process in which water washes chemicals downwards out of the soil. This process is to some degree always taking place around the roots. However, excessive leaching of nitrogen and other minerals not only makes these vital resources unavailable for the tree, but also can pose a danger to the quality of nearby groundwater and streams. There are specific techniques arborists can use to minimize leaching. For instance, arborists should avoid watering loosely packed or sandy soils, should avoid excessive application of fertilizers, and should opt for slow-release and organic fertilizers whenever possible.

23. B: No more than 25 percent of the leaf-bearing crown should be removed during pruning. Removal of large amounts of leaf-bearing branches can lead to decline, especially in older trees. The crown is the upper part of the tree; it begins at the lowest branch, no matter how much lower this branch is than the next-lowest branch. The crown includes all branches and foliage.

24. B: The highly fertile area immediately around growing roots is called the rhizosphere. As the roots grow, they help to create the conditions in which beneficial microorganisms can thrive. Specifically, the roots shed their external layers and release chemicals upon which the microorganisms can feed. Interestingly, the chemical makeup of the rhizosphere is often quite different from that of the immediately adjacent soil. For instance, the pH level in the rhizosphere may be as many as two units higher or lower than the surrounding soil.

25. D: The bare-root trees sold by nurseries are comparatively inexpensive, small, and easy to transplant. These trees are easy to transplant in large part because they have no soil around their root system, making them very light. Typically, bare-root trees perform best when they are planted during the dormant season. The roots must be kept hydrated during the transplantation process. Some of the other varieties of transplant trees may be planted at any time of year.

26. B: In a rigging system the rigging line is usually the weakest component. If the arborist does the working-load limit of the rigging line, he or she can simply ensure that the rest of the equipment is within this limit. The working-load limit, of course, is calculated by dividing the tensile strength by the design factor. In most cases, the default design factor is five.

27. A: Chicago grips are specially designed to be used with extra-high-strength cable. These grips can operate without putting kinks into the cable, so the cable can be used more than one time. A come-along is a tool for pulling two branches together while lag hooks can be installed. The cable is then run between the lag hooks. A Haven grip is appropriate for all cables besides those that are extra strong. A Haven grip is a camming device that enables the climber to attach anchoring equipment.

28. B: The first step in training a young tree is to remove dead or damaged branches. After this, the arborist will select a main branch, or, if the crown of the tree is extremely broad, multiple main branches. The general rule is that the leader should be the strongest and most upright branch on the tree. Selecting a leader helps the arborist to envision the ideal structure of the tree, which will help inform future decisions in the training process. If there are any branches in competition with the selected main branch, these should be cut back to laterals or removed entirely. The arborist will then identify the lowest permanent branch, which should always be less than half of the diameter of the tree at the point of its connection. All of the branches below this branch will be removed. The arborist will then identify the scaffold branches, which will provide the basic lateral structure of the tree. Scaffold branches should be evenly spaced on the trunk. The final step in training a young tree is to select temporary branches among the remaining branches. These branches eventually will be removed, but they should be maintained for the first few years so that they can provide nutrients and shade to the permanent branches and trunk.

29. A: Insects that carry plant pathogens are referred to as vectors. The presence of vectors can turn a relatively minor pest problem into a serious crisis. One common example is Dutch elm disease, which is spread from tree to tree by bark beetles. Nematodes, meanwhile, are tiny, tubular creatures that coexist with plants in both useful and harmful ways. For instance, nematodes are essential in the decomposition of organic material, and some are good at eliminating pests, but others damage the root systems of trees. Galls are irregularly shaped dark patches on the leaves, typically caused by disease, fungus, or bacteria. Herbivores are animals that eat plants only.

30. C: A ship auger should be the drill bit used when installing hardware in a tree. This is true regardless of whether a battery-powered, electric, or gas-powered drill is used. The advantage of the ship auger is that it removes shavings from the hole as it operates and is able to move effectively through green wood. A threaded rod, on the other hand, is a metal rod that supports tree sections or crotches. Threaded rods are also occasionally known as bracing rods.

31. C: Resistance to changes in pH is also known as buffering capacity. A high buffering capacity is associated with soils that have a high proportion of organic matter or clay. In general, it is a good thing for a soil to have a high buffering capacity, because frequent or wild alterations in pH are not good for the soil. There are some basic ways to make slight adjustments to soil pH: for instance, lime will briefly raise the pH, while sulfur creates a temporary decline. Infiltration rate, meanwhile, is the speed with which soil is penetrated by water. Cation exchange capacity is the extent to which soil can absorb and hold positively charged ions. The soil pH has a great influence on the cation exchange capacity. Volatilization, finally, is the translation of a liquid or solid into a vapor or gas.

32. D: A variety is a group within a species that has one trait in complete distinction to the other members of the species and naturally breeds to that trait. Forma, on the other hand, are closely related groups in a species, which occur naturally and in the same geographic area but that have some different traits. For instance, the forma within a particular species may produce differently colored flowers. A subspecies, meanwhile, also occurs naturally, and in the same geographic area as the other members of the species, but it has even greater differences with those other members. Cultivars, finally, are plants that differ from the rest of the plants in their species but that require human effort to grow and produce the desired traits.

33. A: The plant growth regulators that inhibit the work of cell-elongating hormones are called anti-gibberellins. These chemicals can be sprayed on leaves, injected into the tree, or applied to the soil. They have been shown to drastically reduce the growth of the tree, which eliminates the need for frequent and costly pruning. However, there remain concerns about the cytotoxicity of anti-gibberellins, and arborists are advised to use the minimum amount necessary.

34. B: Of the given metrics, cation exchange capacity provides the most accurate indicator of soil fertility. Put simply, cation exchange capacity is the ability of the soil to gather, keep, and trade cations. Soil with a fine texture, or that is high in organic matter and clay, will have a high cation exchange capacity, and will tend to be more fertile. When the soil has a high cation exchange capacity, it is better able to transfer minerals and other nutrients to the roots of the tree.

35. B: Of the given risk assessment techniques, visual tree assessment provides the least information. The visual tree assessment is a systematic appraisal of the external characteristics of the tree. The arborist should be looking for signs of mechanical stress or internal defect. However, this technique is of course limited to the aspects of the tree that can be seen from the outside and is only as comprehensive and insightful as the arborist performing it. In a root collar excavation, on the other hand, soil is removed so that the arborist can investigate the tree's root collar, which is often the place where problems are most evident. In decay testing, the arborist uses a special device to identify rot inside the tree. Finally, in an aerial canopy inspection, the arborist looks at the tree from above and is better able to see problems with the structure of the tree's upper parts.

36. D: Reference evapotranspiration measures the expected amount of plant and soil water loss given location and existing vegetation. The reference evapotranspiration for a given area is expected to remain consistent over time, and figures often are maintained by the local agricultural commission. Moreover, reference evapotranspiration tables often are subdivided so that the precise effects on particular classes of plants may be identified.

37. A: Xeriscaping is intended to protect the landscape against drought. This technique is often used in areas with low or erratic rainfall. There are a few basic components of a xeriscaping strategy. To begin with, the arborist will bring together trees that require similar amounts of rainfall. These groups of trees are known as hydrozones. Xeriscaping will often include the use of low-impact irrigation. The use of water can be minimized by frequently checking soil moisture, both before and after irrigation.

38. B: The post that is attached to the tree and is wrapped in a load line is known as a bollard. Bollards are used to create friction when a load is being lowered. In the past, arborists wrapped the rigging lines around the trunk of the tree, but there are now special devices that make this process a bit easier. In addition, there are bollards in different sizes, which enables the arborist to obtain a superior bend ratio and thereby decrease the amount of strength lost in the rigging line. The bend ratio is the diameter of the bollard relative to the diameter of the rope. A tagline, meanwhile, is a secondary rope that the arborist uses to control the direction in which a branch or tree falls. A kerf is a cut made in a log by a saw. A block, finally, is large pulley, typically used in rigging operations that will include large dynamic loads.

39. C: A tree is said to be a "barber chair" when it splits upward from a back cut. This situation is to be avoided whenever possible, as the split trunk may fall towards the person working on the tree.

40. A: If a chain saw operator loses control of the tree while felling, he or she should move along a line 45-degrees to either side of a line opposite to the intended direction of the fall. Moreover, there should not be any other people in the area immediately behind the tree. Many arborists keep felling wedges on hand while the back cut is being made. If necessary, these wedges can be useful for keeping the tree from pinching the bar of the chain saw. Arborists can also use felling wages to begin and control the fall.

41. C: Workers should stand uphill from the tree while limbing or bucking. This is to prevent the tree from rolling over on the worker. In some cases, the arborist will need to use a wedge or a block to keep the tree from moving. When multiple workers are limbing or bucking the same tree at the same time, they need to be in constant communication, and should have a pre-established system for approaching or alerting one another. Limbing is the process of cutting the side branches off a tree that has been felled. Bucking is the process of cutting a tree trunk or log into shorter sections that are easier to manipulate.

42. A: Groups of different plants that need roughly the same amount of water are called hydrozones. Arborists often arrange trees in hydrozones so that watering is easier and less confusing. In addition, when there are variations in elevation at a particular site, the arborist may place trees that need more water at the higher elevations, so that the trees downhill can subsist entirely on the runoff from the water applied to the higher trees.

43. D: The goal of integrated pest management is to maintain a tolerable level of pest damage. Integrated pest management was originally devised as an alternative to a reliance on pesticides. It recommends a holistic approach to pest control, which may include limited use of pesticides. More importantly, however, integrated pest management strategies create as little of a disturbance to the preexisting environment as possible and prioritize limiting collateral damage to the non-target organisms (most notably, people).

44. C: Heading cuts are used in topping. Topping is an almost universally scorned form of pruning in which the top of the tree is lopped off to a certain height. Besides being aesthetically unpleasant, topping has a number of negative consequences for trees. First, topping drastically reduces the volume of the leaf crown, which makes it extremely difficult for the tree to produce enough food. Topping also makes the tree more susceptible to sun damage, disease, and insect infestation. Finally, topping encourages the growth of numerous weak sprouts from the top of the tree. These water sprouts, as they are known, can put a significant burden on the tree's already-taxed nutritional resources.

45. A: Poison is not a common part of a biological control strategy for pests. In a biological control strategy, the arborist enlists the support of a pest's natural enemies, whether they are predators, parasites, or pathogens. The strategy will take one of three forms: introduction, conservation, or augmentation. That is, the controlling agent may be introduced to the environment so that it can reduce the population of the pest; the existing population of controlling agents may be supported; or the existing population of controlling agents may be supplemented with organisms from the lab or other natural environments. There is an obvious appeal to the idea of using natural means to handle pests, but biological control strategies often are slow and require a great deal of oversight. Moreover, it can be difficult to undo the effects of a biological control strategy.

46. B: A leaf blotch is a large, irregularly shaped area of dead tissue on a leaf. Blotches are typically caused by dryness, frost, fungus, chemical spray, sunscald, or insects. Dieback is the gradual death of leaves and twigs, progressing from the tip back towards the base. It is generally the result of specific nutrient imbalances, air pollution, vascular disease, or root damage. Scorch occurs when leaves turn brown and black and when areas around the leaf edges and margins die. Gummosis is oozing gum or sap from wounds or other openings in the bark.

47. B: Peening is the technique used to keep nuts from backing off in a tree bracing operation. Peening is essentially just hammering the bolt ends so that they expand around the nuts. Propping is a technique for supporting a weak or damaged limb. Guying is another support technique. It is the installation of a cable between a tree and an external object.

48. A: Potassium phosphate is not a standard part of the fertilizer analysis printed on the container. The standard fertilizer analysis includes a breakdown of the total nitrogen, available phosphoric acid, and soluble potash. These quantities are given as a percentage by weight: for instance, a 50-

pound bag of fertilizer listed as 8-5-4 will contain 8 percent nitrogen (4 pounds), 5 percent phosphorus (2.5 pounds), and 4 percent potassium (2 pounds). Complete fertilizers are useful in some cases, but most trees only require nitrogen fertilizer.

49. D: Hardware should be installed along the same line as the pull of the cable. This arrangement maximizes the strength of the hardware. If the cable pulls on the line at an angle, the forces exerted on the hardware will be asymmetrical, and therefore the hardware will not be able to function at its optimal strength.

50. C: Plants that bloom on the wood from the previous season should be pruned just after they bloom, ensuring that blooming buds are not removed from the plant. Although timing is important in the promotion or discouraging of flowers or fruit, it is less significant in the removal of dead, diseased, or broken branches, which can be removed at any time of year.

51. A: During construction, the tree protection zone should extend away from the trunk of a young tree at least 1 foot for each inch of trunk diameter. The tree protection zone is intended to prevent digging and earth moving from adversely affecting the roots. Ideally, the tree protection zone would extend much farther, but at the very least the above guideline should be followed. A larger or older tree would need an even larger protection zone, since its root spread would be much broader.

52. B: Adverse environmental conditions are the most common source of tree problems. Indeed, over 70 percent of all tree problems stem from environmental stressors such as soil compaction, mechanical injury, drought, and extremes of temperature or moisture. Environmental and cultural practices can often have a stronger effect than most insect or pathogen related disorders. However, in most cases environmental stressors are combined with biotic stressors to exacerbate the problem. In particular, trees that have been weakened by environmental problems are often much more susceptible to invasions and infestations by pests.

53. C: Calcium is not necessarily part of a complete fertilizer. A complete fertilizer must include nitrogen, potassium, and phosphorus. Indeed, the standard analysis on the side of a fertilizer container describes the amounts of total nitrogen, available phosphoric acid, and soluble potash. It should be noted that a complete fertilizer is not always an appropriate remedy. For instance, there are many cases in which a tree is deficient only in nitrogen and will benefit more from a fertilizer that focuses on this deficiency only.

54. D: Included bark is commonly found when there are codominant stems. Included bark develops between the stems as bark is pinched between the two growing branches. The presence of included bark makes the branches weaker and can lead to a greater risk of failure in the future. The branch protection zone, meanwhile, is a chemical and physical barrier between the stem and the trunk. A branch protection zone can prevent disease or decay within the branch from reaching the trunk, but it is usually absent when there are codominant stems. A branch collar is an enlarged area at the base of a branch, formed by the overlapping of the branch and trunk bark tissue. The branch collar provides extra support for the branch. A branch bark ridge is a strip of bark atop the branch union, created by the growth of the trunk or the parent stem. Again, this structure will provide extra support, but it is either absent or ineffectively formed when there are codominant stems.

55. D: Slow-release nitrogen fertilizer is recommended for some newly planted trees to encourage root exploration and to provide a steady low-salt nutrient source for establishing trees. Generally, most trees do not need supplementary fertilizer to thrive unless there exist soil conditions that are low in certain nutrients or nutrients are tied up in a form that makes them unavailable to the plant.

56. B: The greenhouse effect is caused by excess amounts of carbon in the atmosphere. Trees, along with other plants, are able to counteract this phenomenon through a process known as carbon sequestration. Carbon dioxide is absorbed into tree tissue, where it remains until the tree dies and decomposes. Trees represent an important element of the carbon cycle.

57. A: Crown restoration may be used to correct the problems created by topping. To restore a crown, the arborist will remove water sprouts, dead branches, and stubs. The arborist will select a few strong branches to be the permanent branches of the new crown. The restoration process does not occur at once: the arborist usually must return to the tree several times over a period of years in order to make the right pruning decisions. Crown cleaning, meanwhile, is the removal of weak, dead, diseased, or broken branches from the tree crown. Crown thinning combines cleaning with the removal of some healthy branches to aid with light infiltration and airflow in a tree canopy. Crown thinning is used mostly for orchard trees and is no longer recognized by ANSI A300 pruning standards as a regular pruning specification for landscape trees. Crown reduction is meant to diminish the overall size of the tree. To reduce the crown, the arborist will cut major limbs back to strong laterals or all the way to the point of origin.

58. B: When moving a heavy object from the ground, the back should be kept in a position of comfort above the lower part of the body. It was long recommended that the back be straight when lifting heavy objects, but recent research has suggested that it may be better to maintain a normal posture, at least in terms of back curvature. Some researchers believe that paying too close attention to the curvature of the back makes people lift primarily with the back rather than the legs, which is a more serious error.

59. B: In a soil profile, the O horizon is on top and is followed in descending order by the A, B, and C horizons. A horizon is a layer of soil. The O horizon is primarily composed of decomposing organic matter. The A horizon contains sand, clay, and silt and is darker than the layers beneath. The B horizon is a mixture of organic material from above and parent material from below. The C horizon is where soil is created from the parent material. The C horizon lies just above the bedrock.

60. C: Both the location and the intended function of the tree determine the height of the lowest permanent branch during structural pruning. Structural pruning is meant to improve the appearance, health, and longevity of the tree by encouraging a healthy and sound growth pattern. The arborist typically will select a dominant leader and identify the main permanent support branches. The arborist may prune away some of the other branches or may leave them for the time being if they will help support the development of the permanent branches. The height of the lowest permanent branch is left to the discretion of the arborist. If the tree is close to a sidewalk or path, the lowest permanent branch may need to be high enough to allow pedestrian traffic. If the tree stands alone, away from pedestrian thoroughfares, then the lowest permanent branch can be lower.

61. A: A close collection of many palm flowers is known as an inflorescence. In some palm trees, inflorescences may consist of many tiny flowers, which in turn means that the tree will produce a large number of fruit. A frond is a palm leaf. Fronds are large and have a segmented leaf structure. Palms are classified as monocots, a group of plants that do not have growth rings or a cambium. The vascular system of a monocot is distributed throughout the stem and protected by parenchymal cells and dense wood fiber. A petiole is the base of a leaf stalk.

62. A: The working-load limit of a rope is always lower than its tensile strength. The working-load limit is the largest load a rope, piece of equipment, or rope assembly should bear during normal operation. The tensile strength of equipment or rope is the lowest force under which failure will occur during normal operation and with a static load. Working-load limit is calculated by dividing the tensile strength by the design factor. The design factor of rope or equipment is a number representing the effects of the particular conditions in which the rope will be used. A high design factor indicates poor conditions, while a low design factor indicates minimal friction and a clean workspace. The standard design factor for arboriculture work under normal conditions is five.

63. B: A turgid leaf is fully hydrated. If the tree is healthy, the leaves should always be turgid in the early morning, even during the hottest part of the year. However, if the tree is dehydrated, the leaves may begin to curl up or yellow slightly.

64. C: Cytokinins are produced in the roots but are crucial for the growth of the shoots. These hormones are in many ways the counterpart to auxin, which is produced in the shoots but is an essential part of root growth. Cytokinins encourage cell division in the shoots.

65. A: The slow process through which a tree becomes accustomed to variations in its environment is called acclimation. Any tree that is to survive conditions unlike those where it originates will have to acclimate. Aggregation, on the other hand, is a gathering together, as of soil particles. In arboriculture, hardening off is the process by which the outermost plant tissue adjusts to a new, often colder environment.

66. C: An ideal soil is composed of 45 percent mineral solids. Mineral solids may include sand, clay, and silt. These components of the soil derived from the parent material, that is, the bedrock underlying the soil. The ideal soil will be halfway made up of pore space, which may be either water or air. The remaining 5 percent of the ideal soil is organic matter and organisms.

67. B: Most trees are excurrent at the beginning of their lives and become more decurrent over time. The excurrent tree grows mostly straight up and typically has a single, dominant, central leader. Conifers are the most classically excurrent trees. A decurrent tree, on the other hand, is rounder and tends to develop stronger lateral branches.

68. A: One advantage of common-grade cable over extra-high-strength cable is that common-grade cable is much more malleable. These are the main two types of cable used for cabling trees. While common-grade cable is more malleable, it is also weaker. For tree work, common-grade and extra-high-strength cable are used in diameters ranging from three-sixteenths to three-eighths inch.

69. B: When attaching a cable to anchoring hardware, thimbles should be used to increase the bend radius of the cable. Arborists should use either stainless steel or galvanized thimble. The purpose of the thimble is to allow the cable to bend a bit more in response to wind or the growth of the tree. Extra-high-strength cable may be used with a thimble when attaching a cable to anchoring hardware, though this cable may also be used without a thimble. Using a thimble should reduce the abrasion on the cable.

70. D: Monocotyledons and dicotyledons are the two classes of angiosperms. An angiosperm is a plant whose seeds are covered by a fruit. Monocotyledons begin life with one seed leaf, while dicotyledons have two. The vast majority of trees are dicotyledons, though palms are monocotyledons. A gymnosperm, on the other hand, has nothing surrounding its seeds. Arboriculture is the study of trees and tree care. Morphology is the study of structure and form of plants and other organisms.

71. C: When multiple cables are installed on the same limb, there should be a minimum of one branch diameter's vertical space between the sets of hardware. Furthermore, there should only be one cable connected to each lag or bolt. The cables need to be inspected regularly and it may be necessary to clear away the brush or the branches near the lags or bolts.

72. A: The base of the leaf stem, before the beginning of the blade, is known as the petiole. The midrib is the spine that runs in between the leaf blades. A leaflet is one of the opposing, smaller leaves on a compound leaf. The petiolule is the base of the leaflet stem.

73. D: The recommended minimum bend ratio for a pulley used as part of a block system in rigging is 4:1. The bend ratio is the relationship between the diameter of the pulley and the diameter of the rope. Having a sufficiently large bend ratio ensures that the blocking system will work properly and that the block and rope will suffer no more than normal wear and tear. Experts also recommend using a braided rope rather than a three-strand rope. A block is a massive pulley that can be used in rigging. It is designed to endure dynamic loading. Arborists should inspect their blocks regularly, as even a small interfering object can quickly damage the rigging line.

74. A: The connecting links used in rigging should be made of steel. Many arborists prefer to use aluminum for climbing, mainly because of its lightness, but it is not strong enough to use in rigging. Because the connecting links used in rigging are often required to bear heavy loads, including dynamic loads, as well as many loading cycles, they must be as strong as possible. An arborist should always check the composition of the connecting links used in rigging, as many connecting links are not strong enough to handle dynamic loads.

75. A: Only one cable should be installed on a single eye bolt or lag. An eye bolt is a cable anchor with a closed eye. Eye bolts are typically machine threaded. In the United States, tree support systems may only employ drop-forged eye bolts.

76. D: Balled-and-burlapped nursery stock has up to 90 percent of its absorbing roots removed before sale. These trees are dug from the ground upon being sold, and the small remaining root ball is wrapped in burlap. In many cases, the tree will actually be planted in a biodegradable burlap, but the top and sides of the burlap should be lowered so that the surface roots may expand easily.

77. D: According to Alex Shigo's model, wall 4 is not a part of the reaction zone. The Shigo model posits four walls that are instrumental in the compartmentalization of decay and injury. Walls 1, 2, and 3 make up the reaction zone, which is what prevents existing decay from spreading throughout the tree. Wall 1 stops up the xylem vessels so that the decay cannot move vertically through the tree. Wall 2 sets up a chemical resistance to the inward spread of decay. Wall 3 works with the ray cells to prevent decay from spreading laterally throughout the tree. Wall 4 is considered to be the barrier zone rather than the reaction zone. It consists of the new growth that follows the injury or decay and that keeps it from spreading outward. Wall 4 is generally stronger and less likely to fail than any of the walls in the reaction zone. Shigo's model is known as CODIT, for Compartmentalization Of Decay In Trees.

78. D: The typical means of attaching common, seven-strand cable to hardware is an eye splice. The eye splice is created by wrapping the end of the cable around the bend in the thimble, separating the strands, and then wrapping them around the cable.

79. C: Class, order, family, and genus are placed in order from general to specific. The full taxonomic hierarchy is kingdom, phylum (sometimes called division), class, order, family, genus, and specific epithet. Arborists often use mnemonics, like Keeping Precious Creatures Organized For Grumpy Scientists, to keep these terms in order. At the highest classification level, all trees are in the plant kingdom. At the phylum level, trees are divided into those that have vascular tissue and those that do not. There are two classes of tree: monocotyledons, which have one seed per leaf, and dicotyledons, which have two. Trees are then further divided by order and family. Trees within the same family tend to have similar fruit and/or flowers. The final two terms, genus and specific epithet, comprise the species name.

80. C: Hardiness is the tree's ability to withstand extremely hot or cold temperatures and other adverse conditions such as drought and flooding. Moderate and temperate temperatures are not a factor when measuring plant hardiness. Temperature extremes are generally damaging to plants, while temperature fluctuations within the acceptable range usually do not cause damage to plants, though they can affect physiological processes. Hardiness is often overlooked characteristic when trees are being selected for transplanting. To improve the ability of arborists to select appropriately hardy trees, the U.S. National Arboretum has created a series of maps indicating the various hardiness zones in North America.

81. D: In arboriculture, a witch's broom is a cluster of weak secondary shoots. A witch's broom is likely to occur after topping or any other aggressive pruning. These shoots are demanding of the tree's resources and produce no branches that will be successful in the long term.

82. A: When installing hardware in a tree, the drilled hole should be about one-sixteenth inch larger than the hardware. This extra diameter makes it possible for the hardware to expand slightly or move a bit without damaging the tree internally. It is always important to drill the hole perpendicular to the section of the tree to which it is connected and such that the hardware will come out straight and not at an angle. This installation practice will increase the longevity of the hardware and the bolt.

83. B: Another name for the outermost rings of the xylem is sapwood. Xylem is the system of vascular structures and wood fibers that provides structural support and transports water and minerals up through the tree. The phloem is the tissue that moves food through a vascular plant. Phloem, which is also known as bast, is composed of fibers, parenchyma, and sieve tubes.

The cambium is the thin layer of cells that produce new tree tissue on each side, externally on the bark and internally in the wood tissue. The heartwood creates a chemical barrier against insects and disease, as well as providing structural support. Not every tree has heartwood.

84. C: A tree that leans toward an area of sunlight is displaying a tropism. A tropism is any movement of a plant in response to a stimulus. There are many different types of tropism. A movement toward the sun would be a heliotropism, while a movement away from the sun would be a paraheliotropism. Trees also display hydrotropism, a movement towards water, and geotropism, a movement towards the center of the earth caused by gravity. In some conditions a plant may perform a thermotropism, which is a movement toward a source of heat other than the sun.

85. B: Of the given types of organic mulch, bark will break down most slowly. The rate of decomposition of a given fertilizer also depends on the climate. In a warm or wet climate, mulch will decompose at a faster pace. An arborist should be conscious of the rate at which mulch will break down, because in some situations it is inconvenient to replace the mulch frequently. When spreading organic mulch, it is better for the material to be broad than deep. At most, the pile of mulch around the tree should be four inches deep. Also, the mulch should not be placed up against the base of the trunk, as this can lead to rot and fungal infections.

86. A: When removing a dead branch, the final cut should be made just outside the collar of living tissue. When removing heavy or large limbs, the arborist should use the three-cut method. The first cut is made one or two feet out on the branch. The arborist will usually make a slight undercut before lopping off the end of the branch from the top. The point of this first move is to drastically reduce the weight of the branch so that the remaining cuts may be made with more precision. After these two cuts have reduced the limb to a stub, the final cut is made just outside the collar of living tissue. The tree will be less damaged by a cut that leaves the living tissue behind.

87. D: The drawing of the soil's nutrients into the atmosphere through transpiration is not a part of nutrient cycling, which is the process through which nutrients infuse the soil and are utilized by living organisms, in this case trees. The soil is full of nutrients, which it obtains from decomposing plants. After some time in the soil, the nutrients are delivered to new plant life, and the cycle continues.

88. A: *Nepenthes* × *hookeriana*, or Hooker's pitcher-plant, is a hybrid. This is denoted by the ×, which should not be placed in italics. A hybrid is a plant that is bred from two different species. Typically, the plants used to produce a hybrid are in the same genus.

89. B: Pest resurgence occurs because indiscriminate pesticide use kills pests and their predators, but when the pesticides cease to be used, the predators take longer to respond than the pests. A pest resurgence often occurs after large-scale and blanket use of pesticides. The arborist should keep in mind that many pests have almost no checks on their population growth and will proliferate exponentially in the absence of natural predators. A similar phenomenon, known as secondary pest outbreak, occurs when the elimination of both pest and predator creates a vacuum into which a new pest may enter and thrive. Arborists should attempt to avoid pest resurgence and secondary pest outbreaks by using narrow-spectrum pesticides in a targeted fashion.

90. B: An arborist would water infrequently but deeply to encourage the development of deep roots. Arborists use different watering strategies to enhance different parts of the root system. In order to improve the roots closest to the surface, an arborist would water a little bit, quite frequently. The deeper roots can be improved by infrequent but thorough watering. The watering must be thorough enough to reach the deep roots but not so often that it drowns the upper roots.

91. D: Removing all of the lateral branches from a felled tree is called limbing. Bucking, on the other hand, is dividing a tree trunk into smaller, more easily manipulated pieces. Pruning and trimming are techniques for removing dead, diseased, decaying, or structurally undesirable branches.

92. A: When two trees are guyed together, the guy on the supported tree should be above the midpoint, and the guy on the anchor tree should be on the lower half of the trunk. If possible, the guy on the supported tree should be about two-thirds of the way up the tree. Before the guying operation is undertaken, however, the arborist should ensure that the supporting tree is strong enough to perform this function. The arborist also must attend to the safety of the guying equipment itself. If the guy wires come loose suddenly, they could pose a grave danger to any person standing nearby. The arborist should ensure that the wood where the guys will be installed is strong enough to hold the bolts.

93. D: A lenticel is a small aperture in the bark, through which gases may travel. These openings are important, because otherwise the bark is covered with oil and wax that prevents the tree from losing water or being exposed to the elements.

94. B: Purple would not be the product of a carotenoid pigment. Instead, purple would be more likely the result of an anthocyanin pigment. These pigments are always present in leaves, but through most of the year they are overwhelmed by the chlorophyll. When the chlorophyll begins to degrade in the late autumn, the other pigments in the leaves will become evident. Specifically, chlorophyll production is diminished by the increase in cold weather.

95. C: The elm is ring porous. This means that at the beginning of the growing season, the new xylem is composed of many large vessels, which gradually diminish over the next few months. The differences in the new wood are the result of the different conditions within the tree as new shoots are produced in the crown. The magnolia, birch, and beech are all diffuse porous, which means that they produce the same small vessels in the xylem throughout the entire growing season. Trees may also be defined as semi-ring porous or semi-diffuse porous. A semi-ring porous tree has just a few large vessels, which gradually diminish in size, while a semi-diffuse porous tree has many small vessels that become even smaller over the course of the growing season.

96. D: At the base of a branch, the branch xylem is oriented downward. From there, the xylem forms a ring around the branch where it meets the trunk. This is the base of the trunk collar. The collar becomes larger when the ring of branch xylem is covered by a ring of trunk xylem. Another layer of xylem is added each year, thus strengthening the trunk collar.

97. A: Brown rot is most likely to be found on a conifer. Brown rot makes wood extremely brittle by degrading the cellulose and isolating the lignin in the wood. Lignin is the substance that provides wood with its compressive strength, but when it becomes overabundant the wood becomes intolerant to any bending at all. The lignin has a dark brown hue, which is why an excessive amount of this substance will result in brown rot.

98. B: Two workers using chain saws at the same time on the same tree should be a minimum of 10 feet apart. This is one of the basic rules of chain saw safety. In addition, the chain saw should always be held on the right side of the body and as close to the lower torso as possible. An arborist should not hold the saw too far away from his or her body, as this reduces control. When more than one worker is using a chain saw at the same time, neither should approach the other without receiving explicit permission. Moreover, no one should approach any chain saw operator from behind.

99. B: Leaf thickness does not affect the extent of damage when lightning strikes a tree. However, the moisture content, wood porosity, and bark thickness can all significantly impact the damage done by lightning. If the tree has high moisture content, the electrical charge will be conducted through the tree easily, and more parts of the tree will be damaged. If the wood is very porous, the tree will be more likely to splinter when it is struck by lightning. Finally, if the bark is thick, the damage to the inside of the tree may not be evident from the outside. In some cases, the bark is so thick that the lightning damage to the vascular tissue of the tree cannot be seen, and it may be too late once the damage finally becomes evident.

100. C: As part of prescription fertilization, an arborist needs to obtain samples from the soil and leaves. Prescription fertilization is the application of a fertilizer targeted at the specific needs of the tree. In order to identify the nutrient deficiencies of the tree, the arborist needs to perform soil and foliar analysis. A standard soil analysis measures the soil pH, salt content, cation exchange capacity, and other important factors. A foliar analysis should include samples from all around the tree.

101. C: The side plates of an arborist block extend beyond the sheaves to prevent abrasion of the line. An arborist block is a durable pulley system that has two sheaves: a small fixed sheave for a rope sling and a large rotating sheave for the lowering line. The side plates of the block are especially long so that the rope will not be damaged by the large amount of friction generated during tree work.

102. A: When looking at a cross section of a branch, the first ring inside the cambium represents the most recent year of growth. The cambium is the narrow layer of meristematic cells whose growth increases the diameter of the stems and roots. The division of the cells in the cambium is responsible for both the production of new bark and new wood tissue. The bark cells are produced on the outside of the cambium ring and the wood cells on the inside. The most recent year of wood tissue growth, then, will be just inside the cambium.

103. D: When an arborist is cutting a branch with the top of the chain saw bar, the saw will tend to push back toward the arborist. Indeed, the outer part of the top of the saw is known as the kickback quadrant for this reason. In order to prevent injury due to kickback, the arborist should take a few basic precautions. To begin with, the arborist should never operate a chain saw above shoulder level. The arborist should never handle the chain saw with one hand, as this will not be sufficient to control the saw should kickback occur by accident. Also, the arborist should be alert to the location of the upper saw tip at all times.

104. C: Either a shackle or a clevis may be used in place of a large screw link. Clevises and shackles are essentially the same thing, a U-shaped fitting in which the gap in the U is filled by a movable pin. Shackles and clevises may be used instead of screw links because they require more than one intentional motion to be opened.

105. A: As water and/or nutrient availability improves, the growth rate increases and the allelochemical concentration decreases. When there is very little water or limited nutrients, the growth rate and the concentration of allelochemicals are both low. If the water for nutrient availability improves slightly, there will be a sufficient amount of carbohydrates to support defense processes but not enough to noticeably increase the growth rate. So, for a brief time, the concentration of defense chemicals will increase much more rapidly than the growth rate. However, once water and/or nutrient availability reaches a tolerable level, the concentration of allelochemicals will begin to drop and the growth rate will begin to rise.

106. D: In legal circumstances, a naturally occurring event that could not have been foreseen or prevented is called an act of God. In most cases, an arborist will not be responsible for damage or injury caused by acts of God. However, neither the arborist nor the owner of the tree will escape liability for injury or damages caused by problems that were known before the event. In other words, the owner of the tree is responsible for monitoring his or her property to ensure that it is safe.

107. B: A nonindigenous species that will propagate without assistance and has become established in a particular area is classified as naturalized. An introduced species is simply one that has been moved into a new area. If an introduced species is successful and thrives for many generations without human intervention, it may be described as naturalized. An invasive species is introduced into a new environment and quickly takes over, driving out the indigenous species and creating problems in the ecosystem. A native species, finally, lives in its original area, to which it is fully adapted.

108. A: Sweating is the process by which bare-root nursery stock is rapidly changed from dormancy to growth. Bare-root nursery stock is often kept in a cold environment until sale. Then it is subjected to a rapid warming process, which takes the tree out of dormancy. At this point, the tree is ready to thrive in its new environment.

109. D: In the open-face notch commonly used in felling, the two cuts form an approximate right angle. The open-face notch is recommended in most cases. It is formed by making two diagonal cuts into the tree, one from above and one from below. A conventional notch is formed by a diagonal cut from above and a horizontal cut. A Humboldt notch is a horizontal cut and a diagonal cut from below. For all of the notch styles, the depth of the notch should typically be a maximum of one-third of the tree's diameter.

110. A: A dormant horticultural oil should be applied before bud break. These oils target harmful pests without eliminating other insects. There are many varieties of dormant horticultural oils, each of which is aimed at a specific class of pest.

111. C: Both extra-high-strength cable and common-grade, seven-strand, galvanized cable are often used for cabling trees. Common-grade, seven-strand, galvanized cable is a form of cable in which seven individual strands are twisted around one another in a spiral. This sort of cable ends by being wrapped upon itself. Extra-high-strength cable also is composed of seven strands, but it is less flexible than common-grade cable. Also, extra-high-strength cable terminates in dead-end tree grips.

112. B: Compost needs to be turned and watered occasionally to maintain sufficient levels of oxygen and water. In a composting operation, organic matter is decomposed by the naturally occurring microorganisms in the soil. Composting is a great idea because it produces an extremely rich soil for gardening. However, in order for this process to be effective, the microorganisms need access to sufficient oxygen and water. Indeed, compost piles often require a great deal of water, because the decomposition generates a great deal of heat, which is useful for eliminating weeds and pathogens but which can quickly dry out the pile.

113. B: The open spaces in plant tissues are called apoplasm. The apoplasm includes the spaces in between the cells as well as the cell walls. The apoplasm may also be defined as the nonliving tissue of the tree. Symplasm, on the other hand, is the living tissue. Both symplasm and apoplasm are part of the xylem.

114. D: An arborist would not install cables to counterbalance a weak root system. It is generally thought that a tree with a weak root system should just be removed and that cable installation will not be sufficient to resolve the tree's problems. Cables may be advantageous in a number of other ways, however. Cables can be used to support the branches that hang over traffic or pedestrian areas, and they also can support decayed or split branches. Cables often are used to support codominant branches with included bark.

115. A: The temporary housing of carbon dioxide in the wood and other tissues of a tree is known as carbon sequestration. The storage of excess carbon dioxide is just one of the benefits trees provide for the environment. When the levels of carbon dioxide become too high, the heat of the sun is trapped in the atmosphere, a phenomenon known as the greenhouse effect. The carbon dioxide that is sequestered in the tree is released when the tree dies and decomposes.

116. B: Phenology is the interaction between changes in weather and recurring biological phenomena. In arboriculture, phenology relates to the times of year when a tree produces or sheds flowers or leaves. Morphology, meanwhile, is the study of the structure and shape of living organisms. Tomography is a process in which waves are sent through an object, and the resulting images give information about the internal structure. Arborists use tomography to inspect trees for decay. Hydrology is the study of water's effects on the Earth's atmosphere and surface.

117. A: In a bight, the rope does not cross over itself. A bight is a curve in between the standing part and the working part of the rope. It is formed by pinching two parts of the rope together, such that a small circle is formed. Loops and turns are both formed by making a circle with the rope, such that the rope crosses over itself. The difference between a loop and a turn is that a turn is used to hold rigging equipment, like carabiners, shackles, and clevises. A round turn entails multiple turns, with a piece of rigging equipment attached to the rope in several places.

118. D: The E horizon is a lighter color than the A horizon because it has less organic material. Not every soil has an E horizon, but in those that do it is found below the A horizon. Because it is farther away from the surface, it contains significantly less organic matter and therefore is much lighter in color. However, both the E and A horizons are included in the general classification of topsoil. Despite containing a great deal of organic material, the A horizon is mostly made up of sand, silt, and/or clay, all of which are inorganic.

119. A: With regard to rope, glazing is melted fiber. Glazing does not have to be caused by open flame or contact with hot objects: it can also be the result of friction. Any rope that is run through a crotch or pulley system quickly or while lifting a heavy object should be checked for glazing, especially if the rope has a tendency to flatten out as it bends around something else.

120. D: Plants that are specially adapted to dry conditions are called xerophytes. Some xerophytes have thicker leaves, while others have less surface area overall, which results in less water lost. Xerophytes may do a good job of conserving water or may have capacious water storage. Cacti are the best example of a xerophyte. Halophytes are plants that grow in salty water, while hydrophytes are plants that can grow in either fresh or saltwater. Finally, mesophytes are adapted to a climate that is neither very dry nor very wet.

121. C: An imbalance in salt can lead to the harmful phenomenon of reverse osmosis. Reverse osmosis occurs when the salt levels in the soil become so high that water is drawn from the roots. This can result in root burn. The salt levels of the soil may become particularly high when certain fertilizers are used.

122. A: A broad planting of the same species over a wide area is known as a monoculture. Many landscape designers plant monocultures because of the ease, but there can be disastrous consequences for the environment. Without variety, the trees are more susceptible to pest infestations and disease. A permaculture is a self-sustaining array of plant life in a particular area. A monocot is a plant, like a grass or a palm, that has only one seed leaf. A pathogen is an organism or substance that causes disease.

123. A: In general, when felling a tree, the hinge should be approximately 80 percent of the diameter of the tree. The hinge is the strip of wood fibers formed between the back cut and the face cut or notch that enables the arborist to control the direction in which the tree or branch falls. Having a larger hinge gives the arborist more control over the direction of the fall.

124. B: Blocks do not create a naturally uneven load on the rope. On the contrary, one of the advantages of using blocks instead of running lines through tree crotches is that it is easier to make the load even. Moreover, using blocks can decrease the wear on the rigging lines, limit the damage to the tree, and decrease the amount of force required to move an object.

125. C: Kernmantle rope always has a cover and a core. The difference between kernmantle and other ropes with a cover and a core is that in kernmantle the yarns that make up the core are twisted rather than braided. Three-strand rope is an extremely simple and relatively weak rope that costs very little. In some situations, it is appropriate to use three-strand rope for climbing or rigging in a natural crotch. Twelve-strand rope comes in both solid-braid and hollow-braid forms. A solid-braid 12-strand rope may be used for natural crotch rigging, but hollow-braid 12-strand rope should not be used for climbing or rigging.

126. D: Of the given macronutrients, a tree is most likely to be deficient in nitrogen. Moreover, nitrogen is the element a tree needs in the largest supply. For this reason, there are a number of nitrogen-specific fertilizers. A complete fertilizer will contain nitrogen, potassium, and phosphorus. Plants require nitrogen for photosynthesis and the formation of proteins. Trees and other plants obtain most of their nitrogen from decomposing plant matter. If a tree does not receive sufficient nitrogen, it may manifest in chlorosis or diminished foliage. Sulfur, phosphorus, and potassium are also defined as macronutrients for trees, meaning that the tree requires these elements in large amounts.

127. A: Heart rot is not a common disease caused by bacteria. Rather, it is caused by a fungus that grows on the open wood or on wounds. Fire blight is a bacterial disease that primarily affects apple, pear, and hawthorn trees. A tree afflicted with fire blight presents with brown foliage and the death of branches. Crown gall is a bacterial disease that afflicts a large number of woody plants and typically appears as an enlarged stem near the roof crown. Bacterial leaf scorch is a disease that clogs the xylem, which causes the leaf margins to turn brown. If allowed to spread throughout the entire crown, bacterial leaf scorch can be fatal to the tree.

128. C: One disadvantage of surface application of fertilizer is that after application, the fertilizer sometimes runs off into nearby bodies of water. Arborists must be careful to avoid surface application of fertilizers in places where runoff is likely. Depending on whether a wet or dry formula is used, the arborist will require a sprayer or a spreader, respectively. In many cases, the arborist will need to water the fertilized area thoroughly so that the fertilizer fully penetrates the soil. The other answer choices are incorrect statements about the surface application of fertilizers. Surface application requires much less time than other methods and does not require complicated or expensive equipment. Moreover, surface application followed by appropriate watering delivers the fertilizer to the top 6 inches of soil, where most of the key roots are found.

129. B: A tree that displays early fall color most likely has problems with its roots. In particular, girdling roots can lead to early fall color. A girdling root crosses over other roots and constricts them. With time, girdling roots can compress the phloem tissues in the trunk and can prevent the roots from delivering water and nutrients to the rest of the tree. Girdling roots usually do not develop by themselves but instead are the result of poor planting or excessive time in a container prior to planting.

130. D: Powdery mildew disease is most prevalent in a warm and dry climate. It is a fungal infection that presents as a dusty, white or gray powder-like substance on the leaves. It tends to be the most prevalent on the lowest leaves. This disease most often affects crabapple, linden, chokeberry, and catalpa trees.

131. A: Poor drainage is a common cause of chronic stress. The other answer choices are common causes of acute stress. In arboriculture, there is an important distinction between chronic and acute stress. Chronic stress develops over a long time and may be difficult to observe in its early stages. It is the result of persistent adverse conditions, like compacted soil, extreme pH, pollution, and malnutrition. Acute stress, on the other hand, occurs in an instant, and the effects are often immediately apparent. Some of the common acute stressors are excessive or inappropriate pesticides, lightning, and frost.

132. B: A tree that has been living in drought conditions should not be treated with fertilizer implants or injections. Implants and injections deliver the fertilizer directly to the xylem. These methods are useful for resolving a specific micronutrient deficiency but should be used sparingly. Trees in drought conditions should not receive implants or injections because active transpiration is required to draw the fertilizer throughout. In addition, arborists should drill small holes in the base of the trunk for the implants or injections.

133. A: A clay loam will have a broader wetting pattern than a sandy loam. The wetting pattern of a clay loam will also be deeper than that of a sandy loam. The downward movement of water through a soil is called infiltration, while the lateral movement is called percolation. In general, a clay soil will have greater infiltration and percolation rates than other soils, although this behavior also may be influenced by the density and structure of the soil. One advantage of clay soils is that they may be watered heavily and all at once, since the water will immediately infiltrate and percolate throughout the soil.

134. A: The generally agreed-upon working-load limit for a new rope used for tree maintenance is 10 percent of the tensile strength. Working-load limit is the maximum static load a rope is asked to bear. If the working-load limit is the same as the tensile strength, the rope could fail on its first use. Therefore, it is necessary to establish a working-load limit that is much smaller than the tensile strength of the rope.

135. C: Sooty mold is based on the liquid waste of mealybugs. This waste, known as honeydew, provides an ideal platform for sooty mold. Mealybugs are often found in hickory or pecan trees, so any tree underneath a pecan or a hickory is especially likely to develop sooty mold. The good news about sooty mold is that its damage to the tree is mainly cosmetic. However, excessive amounts of sooty mold can prevent the tree from getting enough sunlight.

136. A: When climbing along the end of a horizontal branch, the arborist should keep his or her weight on the rope. The limb should not be trusted to bear the weight of the arborist. In order for the arborist to maintain proper weight distribution, the rope needs to be tied in as high as possible. This allows the arborist to move out along the limb without moving the line far from the vertical. Also, if the arborist will need a saw or blade, it should be tied in on a backup line.

137. D: The chemicals that have an adverse effect on some herbivores and pathogens are known as allelochemicals. Tannins and phenols are two of the more common types of allelochemical. Anti-gibberellins are responsible for managing plant growth. Actinomycetes are a type of soil bacteria that are similar to fungi and that are instrumental in the decomposition of organic material. Auxin is the plant hormone that is responsible for growth and development.

138. A: Personal injury is not one of the prerequisites for a claim of negligence. A claim of negligence may arise from a personal injury as well as damage to property. In order for a claim of negligence to be made, however, there must be a clear duty, a failure to fulfill that duty in a reasonable manner, and a clear harm to the plaintiff as a result of this failure to fulfill the duty.

139. D: The part of a rope that is not in use is called the running end. In a rigging line, the lead is the section that runs from the rigging point to the load. The working end is the part of the rope used for climbing and digging. The fall is the part of the rigging line that runs from the anchor point to the rigging point.

140. B: In plant care, vigor is defined as the plant's genetic ability to handle stress, while vitality is its ability to thrive in a particular environment. These two terms are closely related but have slightly different meanings. Whereas vigor is the ability to survive biotic and abiotic stressors, vitality is the extent to which the plant thrives. That is, vitality is related to the plant's growth, while vigor is related to its survival.

141. C: The formula for counting degree days is to subtract the threshold value from the daily average temperature. Degree days are calculated as part of a systematic consideration of the effects of changing temperatures on the pest population. The threshold value is the minimum temperature that will allow for any insect population growth at all. A standard threshold value for tree pests is 50 degrees Fahrenheit (10 degrees Celsius). The daily average temperature is found by adding the daily high and low temperatures and dividing by two. The difference between the threshold temperature and the daily average temperature is the number of degree day units for the day. Biologists keep track of the aggregate number of degree days as spring progresses, and, once the number reaches a predetermined mark, the biologists recommend the use of pesticides or other control tools. There are standard degree day targets for many common pests.

142. A: The shoot tips of a tree produce most of the auxin. Auxin is one of the major plant hormones and growth regulators. Despite being produced in the shoot tips, it is particularly important in the development of the roots. This has led to problems for arborists in the past, because many assumed that insufficient root growth could be balanced out by cutting back the crown. However, the resulting decrease in auxin only exacerbates the problems with root development.

143. C: The edge of the tree crown is also known as the drip line. That is, the drip line is an imaginary boundary on the soil surface that is demarcated by the branch spread of a group of plants or a single plant. In some instances, roots may grow beyond the drip line of the tree.

144. B: With use, the working-load limit of a rope will decrease. The working-load limit is the greatest load a piece of rope or equipment can support when in a new condition. Even when it is used under ideal conditions, a rope will become worn with use. This will inevitably cause its working-load limit to decrease. The working-load limit applies to normal operation. A rope may fail when subjected to a dynamic load smaller than its published working-load limit, or if it is exposed to a harsh bending radius or other improper use.

145. C: When installing cables with eye bolts or threaded rods, metal washers should be used to keep the nut from being pulled through the tree. Arborists should use heavy-duty round washers, which are both thicker and larger than normal washers. In most cases, the washer can be seated right on top of the bark. However, if the bark of the tree is especially thick, it may be appropriate to remove the bark and countersink the washer against the sapwood.

146. A: The load on a piece of rope may change, but the weight of the object creating the load stays the same. Arborists must always distinguish between a dynamic and a static load. A static load remains constant, as the force on the rope remains the same. A dynamic load, however, fluctuates depending on the force being applied to the rope. When the rope is being slackened so that the load can be lowered, the force on the rope may be greater at first. When the rope is being raised, the load will be equal to the weight of the object.

147. C: To avoid salt burn, fertilizers should have a salt index below 50. Fertilizers are salts and have the same potential as table salt to damage plant life. If there is too much salinity in the soil, the roots may lose moisture and wilt. Indeed, the concentration of salt in the soil can get so high that it draws the water out of the roots, a process known as reverse osmosis. A slow-release fertilizer poses less risk of reverse osmosis and therefore salt burn.

148. D: Dutch elm disease spreads through root graft. This is a particularly serious vascular disease, with the ability to bring down large trees in a short time. It is the work of a beetle that breeds in trees that are already afflicted, as well as in stacks of elm logs. A common source of the beetle responsible for Dutch elm disease is stacks of firewood. These beetles burrow into the wood, creating galleries of female beetles and larvae within the bark. The Dutch elm fungus is a byproduct of the proliferation of these beetles. The fungus grows in the elm bark and even within the tunnels created by the burrowing beetles. As the adult beetles emerge from the holes in which they have grown to maturity, they bring the spores of the fungus with them into the outside world. These spores then afflict Dutch elm trees, from root to crown. The fungus spreads through the graft that is natural to the roots of these trees. Once a tree has been infected by Dutch elm disease, all of the leaves above the infection point will quickly wilt. The mycelium and spores of the fungus will infiltrate the vessel structures of the plants, and an oddly colored ring of xylem will appear in the affected stems.

149. C: Reaction wood does not indicate problems with a leaning tree. Reaction wood is supportive tissue grown by the tree to accommodate and support a lean towards sunlight or air. There are many cases in which a leaning tree is perfectly healthy and requires no intervention from the arborist. However, if the soil around the tree is cracked or the roots are raised, it is more likely that the lean has occurred suddenly and recently and is the result of root failure or problems with the soil. Similarly, mounded soil around the base of the tree suggests that the roots are being lifted unnaturally.

150. B: A positively charged ion is called a cation. Calcium, magnesium, sodium, potassium, and hydrogen are common cations in arboriculture. Anions, on the other hand, are negatively charged ions. The roots of a tree must be able to store and exchange the cations of many essential minerals. A soil is hospitable to trees if it has a high cation exchange capacity. Interestingly, the soils with the highest cation exchange capacity are those with the most negatively charged particles. Because opposites attract, these soils are able to attract and hold onto cations.

151. A: Of the given tree cabling configurations, the hub and spoke is the most complex. In a hub and spoke, a large, more stable tree is at the center, and a ring of trees surrounds it. Each tree in the ring is connected to the hub, as well as being connected to the trees on either side of it. The advantages of the hub and spoke are that it can connect several different leaders and can be designed to allow a great deal of movement for each tree. The box and rotary systems are identical: they are often implemented when crown movement is very important. A triangular system is another simple system for tree cabling; like the other cabling configurations, it is most effective when there is adequate vertical spacing between the cables.

152. B: The roots near the surface exhibit the most aggressive growth. In part, this is because the lower roots lie in soil that is less oxygenated and worse at draining. For this reason, when transplanting a tree, an arborist should always make the receiving hole wider at the top. A good rule of thumb is that the hole should be about the width of the root ball at the bottom, and about two or three times the width of the root ball at the top. If the soil is poorly aerated even at the top, it is wise to increase the diameter of the top of the planting hole. In any case, it is essential that the tree not be planted too deeply. Specifically, the hole should never be deeper than the distance from the bottom of the root ball to the trunk flare. Moreover, there should be at least two primary roots from 1 to 3 inches directly below the soil surface.

153. A: The best time to apply a micronutrient spray to trees is just before a period of heavy growth. Micronutrient spray is a form of foliar application that is used to achieve very specific changes in plant nutrition. In most cases, it is not necessary to apply the spray more than once or twice a year. One of the most common examples of a micronutrient spray is a chelated iron spray, which is used to treat iron chlorosis.

154. D: Topography, average rainfall, and soil profile would all affect the microclimate of a location. Topography is the set of landscape contours. Microclimates are small climatic conditions, extending over a range as small as a few feet. A microclimate could be affected by factors like dew, wind, elevation, season, and soil quality. The average temperature, average rainfall, and soil profile are factors that may extend over a larger area, but they still contribute to the microclimates within that larger area.

155. A: Four pounds of nitrogen per thousand square feet of root area is a typical concentration for slow-release supplemental nitrogen fertilizers used under normal conditions. However, an arborist should be alert to the environmental conditions that could require a greater or smaller concentration. For instance, the tree species, health, and age, and soil texture may all affect the choice of fertilizer. Similarly, the form in which the fertilizer is to be applied is often relevant. It is rare, however, for a fertilizer to be applied in a concentration greater than 6 pounds per thousand square feet of root area.

156. B: The midline clove hitch is primarily used for sending equipment up to a climber. It is popular for this purpose because it can be rapidly tied in the bight of a line. The running bowline, on the other hand, is more often used in tying off limbs. The running bowline acts like a slipknot, in that it can be sent up a line by a person at the end. Moreover, even after it has been loaded, the running bowline is still easy to untie. The figure-eight is a quick and easy stopper knot. Finally, the endline clove hitch is primarily used to secure limbs or trunk pieces. It is an easy knot to master.

157. D: The typical treatment for highly sodic soil is irrigation with low-sodium water. A sodic soil has too much of the cation sodium in its cation exchange capacity. Irrigation with low-sodium water will effectively rinse this cation out of the soil. If the soil is not treated, it could lead to elevated pH levels, nutrient imbalances, crusting, and even sodium levels that threaten some plants. If irrigation with low-sodium water does not work, an arborist may need to add calcium to the soil, typically through the application of gypsum.

158. D: Codominant stems are two stems with roughly equal size that grow from the same place. Codominance is not a desirable trait, because the union between the stems is typically quite weak. Codominant stems lack a branch bark ridge and do not form a branch collar. In other words, the area at the base of the stems is less fortified than it would be if there were a single dominant stem. Also, codominant stems are more likely to have included bark, which is lodged between the stems, creating a structural weakness prone to failure.

159. C: Drop starting is not a recommended method of starting a chain saw. Drop starting is pulling the starter cord while pushing the saw away from the body. One reason why drop starting is not recommended is that it creates an opportunity for the operator to come into contact with a moving chain. In the leglock method, the saw is positioned behind the right knee. This technique is sometimes used in favor of simply starting the saw with it lying on the ground, which is the safest method.

160. D: A battery is not part of a lightning protection system. A lightning protection system must include an air terminal, ground terminal, and set of conductors. The purpose of the system is to divert the electrical energy from lightning away from the tree. The air terminal is placed at the top of the tree, and the conductors run down the central branches to the trunk and then down to the ground. The conductors are typically made of copper, which allows for the easy passage of electricity. It will be necessary to attach the conductor to the tree every few feet. It is only necessary to install one conductor if the diameter of the tree crown is less than 35 feet; broader trees may need secondary conductors along a few of the main branches. These secondary conductors should connect to the main conductor. The main conductor connects to a ground terminal, which typically consists of a set of rods or plates. The ground terminal should not be placed within 2 feet of underground installations or structures. The ground terminal should be at least 8 inches deep underground.

161. C: In the CTLA trunk formula method, the primary determinant of a tree's value is size. The CTLA approach was created by the Council of Tree and Landscape Appraisers. It is important to distinguish between the trunk formula method composed by the CTLA and the CTLA methodology, which is a more holistic assessment rubric for tree health. The CTLA methodology combines scores related to location, species, size, and condition when assessing a tree.

162. A: When applying fertilizer with the drill-hole method, the concentric rings of holes should extend at least to the drip line. The drill-hole method is typically used with granular fertilizer, which will work more quickly when it is placed beneath the soil surface. The arborist will drill holes in concentric circles or in a grid, beginning a few feet out from the trunk and extending at least to the drip line. The holes usually have a diameter of between 2 and 4 inches and are between 1 and 3 feet apart. No holes are placed near the trunk of the tree because excessive fertilizer in this area may damage the buttress roots. The holes are usually between 4 and 8 inches deep. After the holes have been drilled, the arborist will fill them with fertilizer to within 2 inches of the top. In some cases, the arborist will fill in the rest of the hole with sand, bits of stone, or peat moss.

163. B: The appropriate minimum diameter for a main branch used for tying in is 4 inches. The arborist must use a great degree of care when selecting the branches through which to throw the rope. To begin with, the arborist should attempt to select a location where the rope line will be as vertical as possible, as this will diminish the extent to which the arborist could swing from side to side. Moreover, the arborist needs to make sure that he or she doesn't position the rope such that the climber could swing into power lines or another hazard. There should be sufficient room within the crotch for the rope to pass easily. Four inches is the generally accepted diameter, but the branch may need to be larger depending on the strength of the wood.

164. D: The difference between an open and a closed throwing knot is that the open knot will come undone when the rope is thrown. Depending on the situation, either an open or a closed knot may be required. If the arborist needs the rope to descend so that equipment can be attached, an open knot would be better. On the other hand, a closed throwing knot might be appropriate if the arborist wants to have it catch in the crotch or be caught by a climber in the tree.

165. A: In structural pruning, the process of reducing competing stems into laterals is known as subordination. There are many disadvantages to codominant branches, so the arborist will try to preclude this problem by reducing the size and growth of one branch relative to the other. Hardening off, on the other hand, is the process through which a plant tissue becomes adapted to a new environment or to a colder climate. Heading is the pruning technique of cutting a shoot back to the bud or cutting a branch back to its lateral, bud, or stub. This is typically done for structural reasons. Raising is the term in arboriculture for cutting off lower branches in order to increase the vertical clearance around the base of the tree.

166. B: A leaf that displays chlorosis is deficient in chlorophyll. Chlorophyll is responsible for the green color of plants and is a necessary part of photosynthesis. When a plant does not have enough, its green parts may turn yellow or white. The lack of chlorophyll is often the result of disease or malnutrition.

167. C: When planting a large tree, it is a bad idea to fill the bottom of the hole with gravel because the soil can become excessively saturated. This is known as a perched water table, and it can be fatal for trees. If the bottom of the hole is filled with gravel and the rest of the hole is filled in with loose soil, water will sit in the top part of the soil, along with the roots, without ever draining. If this condition is allowed to persist, the roots can drown.

168. D: Galls are irregular plant growths, often found in the leaf tissue. Galls may be the result of any number of pests, including mites, nematodes, bacteria, and fungi. Blotches and spots are both patches of dead tissue on the foliage, though blotches are larger than spots. Leaf scorch is browning and death in between the leaf veins or along the edges of the leaf.

169. C: In a pinnate arrangement of a compound leaf, the leaflets are placed along a single stem, but with a petiole for each leaflet. A pinnate leaf looks a bit like a feather, with a central spine and symmetrical elements laid out around it. Most pinnate leaves are compound, meaning that they are composed of several leaflets. A bipinnate leaf is doubly divided: that is, a bipinnate leaf is composed of several pinnate leaves that emerge from another central axis. A palmate leaf has three or more nerves, leaflets, or lobes originating from a common point.

170. D: The difference between simple and compound leaves is that a simple leaf has a single leaf blade, while a compound leaf may have several leaflets. There are many varieties of both simple and compound leaves. A simple leaf may have lobes, serrations, or both. A compound leaf may have a group of leaflets extending from the same stem or leaflets extending from a series of petioles.

171. B: Urea formaldehyde is a synthetic organic fertilizer. It is composed of both bound and free urea, which means that some of the urea is available at once, while the rest will become available over time. The fertilizer is spread over the target area and then watered into the soil. Microorganisms will convert the urea into ammonium and nitrates. It is important that some of the urea be converted into ammonium, because, unlike urea, this chemical cannot be leached from the soil by heavy rains. An organic fertilizer will disperse its nutrients much more slowly than an inorganic fertilizer, because it operates through the decomposition of its carbon-based materials. The ions released by an organic fertilizer are actually inorganic and are easily absorbed by the roots. Another common synthetic (that is, man-made) organic fertilizer is isobutylidene diurea. Some of the common natural organic fertilizers are bone meal, blood, fish hydrolysates, sewage, and manure.

172. D: A cultivar is a variety that must be grown by humans and that needs human attention to perpetuate a particular trait. In other words, these plants require asexual propagation. The products of this cultivation will be clones with identical genes. A variety, on the other hand, will naturally breed with a trait that distinguishes it from the other members of its species. Creating a variety does not require human intervention. Forma are plants that are subtly different from members of their own species. For instance, a form might have a slightly better or worse response to environmental conditions than other, similar plants. Forma occur naturally. A subspecies also occurs naturally, but its differences with the members of its species are much more profound.

173. A: A loose-weave, hollow-braid, polyester 12-strand rope would be appropriate for rigging slings. However, this rope would not be strong enough for rigging or climbing purposes. A 12-strand rope typically does not have a core. The extent to which such a rope will remain round when bent depends on the diameter of the strands and the pattern of the weave. If the rope flattens out when it is wrapped around an object, it will create more friction and suffer more abrasion.

174. B: Maple, ash, dogwood, and horse chestnut are the main genera of trees that have an opposite leaf arrangement. Arborists often remind themselves of this fact with the mnemonic MAD Horse: that is, Maple, Ash, Dogwood, and Horse chestnut. When a tree has compound leaves, the arborist should distinguish opposite and alternate leaf and bud arrangements according to the position of whole leaves rather than leaflets. In an opposite leaf arrangement, leaves emerge from either side of the stem at exactly the same place. The alternate leaf arrangement also features leaves on either side of the stem, but these leaves emerge at different places along the length of the stem.

175. C: A pine fascicle sheath usually does not contain four needles. A pine fascicle sheath is a close cluster or bundle of needles. The sheath itself is composed of bud scales.

176. B: The tautline hitch is the most popular climbing hitch for climbers in the United States. It is used as a climbing hitch, which means it depends on friction for control. It does require a stopper knot, usually in the form of a figure-eight knot. One of the disadvantages of a tautline hitch is that it tends to roll out. Also, tautline hitches require frequent adjustment. The Blake's hitch is gaining popularity as climbers notice that it maintains a more consistent level of friction and requires less adjustment. Also, a Blake's hitch doesn't roll out as often, though a stopper knot is still advised. A Blake's hitch is more likely to glaze when it is subjected to fast, long descents. The midline clove hitch is generally used to send equipment to a climber above. It is preferred by arborists because it is easy to tie into a bight of a line. An endline clove hitch is often used to tie off sections of wood or limbs. It is typically finished off with two half hitches. The advantage of the endline clove hitch is that it is easy to tie.

177. A: Lignin makes wood resistant to compression. It is found inside the wood cells as well as between them. Some types of fungus, such as white rot, decay lignin, which can make the tree much more susceptible to breaking. Indeed, the name of white rot itself is based on the loss of lignin, as the tree will take on a much lighter hue after the dark lignin is decayed.

178. D: The working-load limit of a rope is calculated by dividing the tensile strength by the design factor. Tensile strength is the minimum force that will immediately break the rope. The tensile strength of a rope will diminish over time. The design factor is a subjective measure of the extent to which the strength of the rope will be compromised. If the rope must hold a dynamic load in poor conditions, the design factor will be high. In arboriculture, the standard design factor for normal conditions is five. So, if a rope has a tensile strength of 10,000 pounds and a design factor of five, the working-load limit of the rope will be 2000 pounds. Cycles to failure, meanwhile, is the number of lifts and drops a rope can endure under normal conditions before it can no longer be used.

179. B: A stem with good taper is less likely to break when subjected to a force. When arborists refer to taper, they mean the gradual decrease in the diameter of the stem from base to tip. The taper of a stem or branch depends on the amount of wind and the proximity of other trees. Trees that grow in dense populations tend to have poor taper. When a tree has good taper, any load it endures will be better distributed, and the tree is less likely to be damaged.

180. C: In a command-and-response system, the climber should move up the tree after he or she has heard an acknowledgement. In the traditional script, the warning is "Stand clear" and the acknowledgment is "All clear." Another standard part of the command-and-response system is that ground workers must receive permission from the climber before entering the landing zone. If background noise makes it impossible to communicate verbally, the workers will need to use a pre-established set of hand signals.

181. A: An integrated pest management system would not classify an organism as a pest simply because it requires intervention. Indeed, many of the insects that are classified as pests by the integrated pest management system do not need to be treated immediately. One of the signature features of IPM is that it considers context: the same organism may be defined as a pest in one situation but not in another. In general, an organism is considered a pest if it competes with desirable plants for nutrients and water. Similarly, an organism that endangers the health or appearance of a desired plant will be considered a pest. Indeed, any organism that decreases the utility, safety, or recreational viability of a tree may be considered a pest.

182. A: It is appropriate to use climbing spurs when the tree is going to be removed. Climbing spurs, otherwise known as climbing spikes, attach to the sole of the boot and drastically improve climbing ability. However, they also leave holes in the bark, which besides being ugly can contribute to pest infestations. When it is necessary to use spurs, the arborist should be tied in with a climbing line or should use a work-positioning lanyard.

183. B: Rays are the radial planes of living cells that extend through the phloem and xylem. The rays move carbohydrates and other nutrients into the sapwood. The heartwood is the innermost part of the xylem; it is composed of dead, nonconducting tissue. Vessels are the hardwood's best conductors. The cambium is a thin layer of cells that produces all of the components of the plant's vascular system.

184. C: In most living trees, the heartwood is dead. The heartwood is the older, nonliving central wood of the tree. The sapwood is the outermost portion of the wood cylinder. In most cases, the sapwood is a lighter color and less dense than the heartwood. The cells on the inside of the sapwood that grow old and die are converted into heartwood. The sapwood is able to conduct water through the tree. Whereas the heartwood of the tree will increase with age, the sapwood maintains a consistent thickness. The cambium, meanwhile, is the layer between the bark and the wood of a tree or other vascular plant. The cambium is usually about an inch thick. The growth of the cambium is in essence the growth of the tree, as the cambium supplies new wood cells on its internal side and new bark on its external side. It is this annual production by the cambium that gives rise to the concentric rings visible in the trunk when a tree is bisected. The xylem is the largest component of the tree. It consists of long, tubular cells that enable the circulation of nutrient-rich water.

185. A: If a tree has an especially large diameter, the hinge should be smaller. The hinge is the point from which the arborist may control a tree that he or she is attempting to fell. In a normal-sized tree, the hinge is usually just about 10 percent of the tree's diameter. However, in a larger tree, it may be that a hinge of this size will not work correctly. In general, a hinge should be approximately 80 percent of the diameter of the tree. The arborist should make certain to avoid compromising the hinge while the back cut is being made.

186. C: On a chain saw, the upper part of the guide bar tip is also known as the kickback quadrant. This is because the saw will tend to push back towards the user when contact is made with the top of the bar. This kickback can happen extremely quickly, so the arborist must always be conscious of the kickback quadrant when using a chain saw. Moreover, the operator should always position himself or herself such that kickback would not cause the saw to hit him or her. Finally, an arborist should never operate a chain saw above the level of his or her shoulders, as this will amplify the damage that can be done by kickback.

187. B: The insect's mouthparts determine the type of damage it will do to a tree. For instance, some insects only chew on leaves, others consume the leaf margins exclusively, and some eat the entire leaf. Some insects bore into the trunks of trees and eat the xylem, cambium, and phloem. Finally, some insects use their sharp mouthparts to pierce the leaves and suck out the liquid within. In this last case, the damage done to the tree may be difficult to see until it is almost too late.

188. D: In the ANSI standards, *should* indicates a recommendation. The terminology used in the ANSI standards is systematic. For instance, when the standards indicate that something is *approved*, this means that it has been judged acceptable by whichever authority has jurisdiction. In addition, the word *shall* indicates an absolute and enforced requirement. *Shall* is a stronger word than *should* in the ANSI standards.

189. B: The optimal level of pore space in a soil is 50 percent. The pore spaces are the parts of soil that contain the oxygen and water, which tree roots need to survive and thrive. When the soil is compacted, the root tips cannot find enough pore space to stimulate their growth.

190. C: A sheet bend would be the best knot for binding two ropes with different diameters. When tying a sheet bend, the smaller rope should be tucked under its own standing part. A Prusik hitch is a friction hitch that can be used for either rigging or climbing. For some of its uses, it is bidirectional. When the Prusik hitch is used as a Prusik loop, it must be attached to the working line with a thinner rope. This technique is used sometimes in secured footlocking. The double fisherman's knot is almost always used to form a Prusik loop. However, the double fisherman's knot can become very difficult to undo after it has been loaded. Finally, the cow hitch with half hitch is often used along with a sling to attach hardware to a tree. This knot system is similar to the simple girth hitch, though it employs a line rather than a loop.

191. B: Bare-root trees are the least susceptible to girdling roots upon planting. A bare-root tree is transplanted without any soil or container surrounding the roots. The tree is usually very young, and the roots are very thin. As long as they are spread out and planted properly, there is little risk of girdling roots. A balled-and-burlapped, containerized, or container-grown tree, on the other hand, will have more developed roots in a restrictive environment, which raises the risk of roots circling back on themselves and constricting others.

192. C: The minimum tensile strength for the snaps and carabiners used in climbing is 5000 pounds. Moreover, the carabiners must be positive locking and self-closing. To be positive locking, carabiners must require more than one motion to open. To be self-closing, they must be capable of locking without any voluntary assistance from the user. The arborist should also be sure to check the status of the carabiners and snaps before they are used, as well as while they are being used.

193. A: Most new roots are white. When selecting a tree for transplant, it is especially important for the arborist to inspect the roots, because the ability of the tree to thrive in its new environment will depend in large part on its ability to live off of stored carbohydrates and immediately begin absorbing water. Whiteness is a strong indicator of root health. It is also important to determine whether the roots are arranged properly and that they are not encircling the stem.

194. C: When a tree has substantial decay on one side, the back cut should be finished on the undecayed side of the tree. If the initial cut is made on the undecayed part of the tree, there is a possibility that the tree will collapse in an unexpected direction. Whenever possible the overall weight of the tree should be diminished through pruning higher up the tree.

195. B: The acronym CODIT stands for Compartmentalization Of Decay In Trees. The CODIT model was developed by Alex Shigo to explain the process by which a tree is able to restrict the spread of decay and disease. Shigo identified four mechanisms, known as walls, through which the tree blocks the expansion of harmful elements in every direction.

196. B: In a small tree, there should be approximately 1 foot of vertical space between scaffold branches. For larger trees, there may need to be as much as 18 vertical inches between scaffold branches. Scaffold branches should be well attached and evenly distributed through the trunk. These branches will outline the structure of the tree.

197. D: The bud at the end of a twig is known as the terminal bud. The previous year's terminal bud should be visible as a band around the circumference of the twig. The amount of growth that has occurred during the year can be determined by measuring the distance from the tip of the terminal bud to the band marking the prior year's terminal bud. Axillary and lateral buds are both found along the side of the twig. Lateral and axillary buds may become flowers, leaves, or twigs. A node, meanwhile, is a fatter part of the stem, from which either leaves or buds may grow.

198. B: A tensiometer measures soil moisture. A tensiometer is composed of a large tube with tiny holes poked in it, inside of which there is a tube filled with water and a pressure sensor. The device measures the extent to which water from the soil permeates the tube and registers pressure on the sensor. Some scientists describe a tensiometer as measuring the "soil moisture tension."

199. C: The process through which leaves lose water vapor is called transpiration. There are a few benefits of transpiration. For one thing, the motion of the water and air helps to cool the leaf. Also, as water passes out of the leaf, more water is brought up through the xylem, which keeps the tree hydrated with fresh water. The broader and flatter the leaf, the more effective will be the process of transpiration. The rate of transpiration also is affected by the temperature and humidity as well as by the amount of available water in the soil. Plants that are adapted to hot and dry climates will often have small, thick leaves, which resist transpiration.

200. A: Frass is a combination of insect waste and sawdust. The presence of frass is often an indicator that something is wrong with the tree. However, frass does have some utility for trees. It stimulates blooming and contains helpful bacteria, fungi, and amoebae. Frass also contributes to nutrient cycling.

FREE Study Skills DVD Offer

Dear Customer,

Thank you for your purchase from Mometrix! We consider it an honor and privilege that you have purchased our product and want to ensure your satisfaction.

As a way of showing our appreciation and to help us better serve you, we have developed a Study Skills DVD that we would like to give you for <u>FREE</u>. **This DVD covers our "best practices" for studying for your exam, from using our study materials to preparing for the day of the test.**

All that we ask is that you email us your feedback that would describe your experience so far with our product. Good, bad or indifferent, we want to know what you think!

To get your **FREE Study Skills DVD**, email <u>freedvd@mometrix.com</u> with "FREE STUDY SKILLS DVD" in the subject line and the following information in the body of the email:

    a. The name of the product you purchased.

    b. Your product rating on a scale of 1-5, with 5 being the highest rating.

    c. Your feedback. It can be long, short, or anything in-between, just your impressions and experience so far with our product. Good feedback might include how our study material met your needs and will highlight features of the product that you found helpful.

    d. Your full name and shipping address where you would like us to send your free DVD.

If you have any questions or concerns, please don't hesitate to contact me directly.

Thanks again!

Sincerely,

Jay Willis
Vice President
<u>jay.willis@mometrix.com</u>
1-800-673-8175

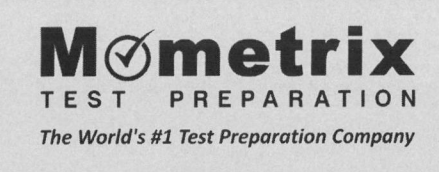

Image Credits

LICENSED UNDER CC BY 4.0 (CREATIVECOMMONS.ORG/LICENSES/BY/4.0/)

Soil Profile: "Horizons" by Wikimedia user Wilsonbiggs (https://commons.wikimedia.org/wiki/File:Horizons.gif)

Structural Soil: "Planting island detail" by Nina Bassuk, PhD (https://blogs.cornell.edu/urbanhort/outreach/cu-structural-soil/cu-structural-soil-graphics-and-plan-views/)

LICENSED UNDER CC BY 3.0 (CREATIVECOMMONS.ORG/LICENSES/BY/3.0/)

Leaf Morphology: "Chart of leaf morphology characteristics" by Wikimedia user Debivort (https://commons.wikimedia.org/wiki/File:Leaf_morphology.svg)

How to Overcome Test Anxiety

Just the thought of taking a test is enough to make most people a little nervous. A test is an important event that can have a long-term impact on your future, so it's important to take it seriously and it's natural to feel anxious about performing well. But just because anxiety is normal, that doesn't mean that it's helpful in test taking, or that you should simply accept it as part of your life. Anxiety can have a variety of effects. These effects can be mild, like making you feel slightly nervous, or severe, like blocking your ability to focus or remember even a simple detail.

If you experience test anxiety—whether severe or mild—it's important to know how to beat it. To discover this, first you need to understand what causes test anxiety.

Causes of Test Anxiety

While we often think of anxiety as an uncontrollable emotional state, it can actually be caused by simple, practical things. One of the most common causes of test anxiety is that a person does not feel adequately prepared for their test. This feeling can be the result of many different issues such as poor study habits or lack of organization, but the most common culprit is time management. Starting to study too late, failing to organize your study time to cover all of the material, or being distracted while you study will mean that you're not well prepared for the test. This may lead to cramming the night before, which will cause you to be physically and mentally exhausted for the test. Poor time management also contributes to feelings of stress, fear, and hopelessness as you realize you are not well prepared but don't know what to do about it.

Other times, test anxiety is not related to your preparation for the test but comes from unresolved fear. This may be a past failure on a test, or poor performance on tests in general. It may come from comparing yourself to others who seem to be performing better or from the stress of living up to expectations. Anxiety may be driven by fears of the future—how failure on this test would affect your educational and career goals. These fears are often completely irrational, but they can still negatively impact your test performance.

Review Video: 3 Reasons You Have Test Anxiety
Visit mometrix.com/academy and enter code: 428468

Elements of Test Anxiety

As mentioned earlier, test anxiety is considered to be an emotional state, but it has physical and mental components as well. Sometimes you may not even realize that you are suffering from test anxiety until you notice the physical symptoms. These can include trembling hands, rapid heartbeat, sweating, nausea, and tense muscles. Extreme anxiety may lead to fainting or vomiting. Obviously, any of these symptoms can have a negative impact on testing. It is important to recognize them as soon as they begin to occur so that you can address the problem before it damages your performance.

> **Review Video: 3 Ways to Tell You Have Test Anxiety**
> Visit mometrix.com/academy and enter code: 927847

The mental components of test anxiety include trouble focusing and inability to remember learned information. During a test, your mind is on high alert, which can help you recall information and stay focused for an extended period of time. However, anxiety interferes with your mind's natural processes, causing you to blank out, even on the questions you know well. The strain of testing during anxiety makes it difficult to stay focused, especially on a test that may take several hours. Extreme anxiety can take a huge mental toll, making it difficult not only to recall test information but even to understand the test questions or pull your thoughts together.

> **Review Video: How Test Anxiety Affects Memory**
> Visit mometrix.com/academy and enter code: 609003

Effects of Test Anxiety

Test anxiety is like a disease—if left untreated, it will get progressively worse. Anxiety leads to poor performance, and this reinforces the feelings of fear and failure, which in turn lead to poor performances on subsequent tests. It can grow from a mild nervousness to a crippling condition. If allowed to progress, test anxiety can have a big impact on your schooling, and consequently on your future.

Test anxiety can spread to other parts of your life. Anxiety on tests can become anxiety in any stressful situation, and blanking on a test can turn into panicking in a job situation. But fortunately, you don't have to let anxiety rule your testing and determine your grades. There are a number of relatively simple steps you can take to move past anxiety and function normally on a test and in the rest of life.

> **Review Video: How Test Anxiety Impacts Your Grades**
> Visit mometrix.com/academy and enter code: 939819

Physical Steps for Beating Test Anxiety

While test anxiety is a serious problem, the good news is that it can be overcome. It doesn't have to control your ability to think and remember information. While it may take time, you can begin taking steps today to beat anxiety.

Just as your first hint that you may be struggling with anxiety comes from the physical symptoms, the first step to treating it is also physical. Rest is crucial for having a clear, strong mind. If you are tired, it is much easier to give in to anxiety. But if you establish good sleep habits, your body and mind will be ready to perform optimally, without the strain of exhaustion. Additionally, sleeping well helps you to retain information better, so you're more likely to recall the answers when you see the test questions.

Getting good sleep means more than going to bed on time. It's important to allow your brain time to relax. Take study breaks from time to time so it doesn't get overworked, and don't study right before bed. Take time to rest your mind before trying to rest your body, or you may find it difficult to fall asleep.

> **Review Video: The Importance of Sleep for Your Brain**
> Visit mometrix.com/academy and enter code: 319338

Along with sleep, other aspects of physical health are important in preparing for a test. Good nutrition is vital for good brain function. Sugary foods and drinks may give a burst of energy but this burst is followed by a crash, both physically and emotionally. Instead, fuel your body with protein and vitamin-rich foods.

Also, drink plenty of water. Dehydration can lead to headaches and exhaustion, especially if your brain is already under stress from the rigors of the test. Particularly if your test is a long one, drink water during the breaks. And if possible, take an energy-boosting snack to eat between sections.

> **Review Video: How Diet Can Affect your Mood**
> Visit mometrix.com/academy and enter code: 624317

Along with sleep and diet, a third important part of physical health is exercise. Maintaining a steady workout schedule is helpful, but even taking 5-minute study breaks to walk can help get your blood pumping faster and clear your head. Exercise also releases endorphins, which contribute to a positive feeling and can help combat test anxiety.

When you nurture your physical health, you are also contributing to your mental health. If your body is healthy, your mind is much more likely to be healthy as well. So take time to rest, nourish your body with healthy food and water, and get moving as much as possible. Taking these physical steps will make you stronger and more able to take the mental steps necessary to overcome test anxiety.

> **Review Video: How to Stay Healthy and Prevent Test Anxiety**
> Visit mometrix.com/academy and enter code: 877894

Mental Steps for Beating Test Anxiety

Working on the mental side of test anxiety can be more challenging, but as with the physical side, there are clear steps you can take to overcome it. As mentioned earlier, test anxiety often stems from lack of preparation, so the obvious solution is to prepare for the test. Effective studying may be the most important weapon you have for beating test anxiety, but you can and should employ several other mental tools to combat fear.

First, boost your confidence by reminding yourself of past success—tests or projects that you aced. If you're putting as much effort into preparing for this test as you did for those, there's no reason you should expect to fail here. Work hard to prepare; then trust your preparation.

Second, surround yourself with encouraging people. It can be helpful to find a study group, but be sure that the people you're around will encourage a positive attitude. If you spend time with others who are anxious or cynical, this will only contribute to your own anxiety. Look for others who are motivated to study hard from a desire to succeed, not from a fear of failure.

Third, reward yourself. A test is physically and mentally tiring, even without anxiety, and it can be helpful to have something to look forward to. Plan an activity following the test, regardless of the outcome, such as going to a movie or getting ice cream.

When you are taking the test, if you find yourself beginning to feel anxious, remind yourself that you know the material. Visualize successfully completing the test. Then take a few deep, relaxing breaths and return to it. Work through the questions carefully but with confidence, knowing that you are capable of succeeding.

Developing a healthy mental approach to test taking will also aid in other areas of life. Test anxiety affects more than just the actual test—it can be damaging to your mental health and even contribute to depression. It's important to beat test anxiety before it becomes a problem for more than testing.

Review Video: Test Anxiety and Depression
Visit mometrix.com/academy and enter code: 904704

Study Strategy

Being prepared for the test is necessary to combat anxiety, but what does being prepared look like? You may study for hours on end and still not feel prepared. What you need is a strategy for test prep. The next few pages outline our recommended steps to help you plan out and conquer the challenge of preparation.

STEP 1: SCOPE OUT THE TEST

Learn everything you can about the format (multiple choice, essay, etc.) and what will be on the test. Gather any study materials, course outlines, or sample exams that may be available. Not only will this help you to prepare, but knowing what to expect can help to alleviate test anxiety.

STEP 2: MAP OUT THE MATERIAL

Look through the textbook or study guide and make note of how many chapters or sections it has. Then divide these over the time you have. For example, if a book has 15 chapters and you have five days to study, you need to cover three chapters each day. Even better, if you have the time, leave an extra day at the end for overall review after you have gone through the material in depth.

If time is limited, you may need to prioritize the material. Look through it and make note of which sections you think you already have a good grasp on, and which need review. While you are studying, skim quickly through the familiar sections and take more time on the challenging parts. Write out your plan so you don't get lost as you go. Having a written plan also helps you feel more in control of the study, so anxiety is less likely to arise from feeling overwhelmed at the amount to cover.

STEP 3: GATHER YOUR TOOLS

Decide what study method works best for you. Do you prefer to highlight in the book as you study and then go back over the highlighted portions? Or do you type out notes of the important information? Or is it helpful to make flashcards that you can carry with you? Assemble the pens, index cards, highlighters, post-it notes, and any other materials you may need so you won't be distracted by getting up to find things while you study.

If you're having a hard time retaining the information or organizing your notes, experiment with different methods. For example, try color-coding by subject with colored pens, highlighters, or post-it notes. If you learn better by hearing, try recording yourself reading your notes so you can listen while in the car, working out, or simply sitting at your desk. Ask a friend to quiz you from your flashcards, or try teaching someone the material to solidify it in your mind.

STEP 4: CREATE YOUR ENVIRONMENT

It's important to avoid distractions while you study. This includes both the obvious distractions like visitors and the subtle distractions like an uncomfortable chair (or a too-comfortable couch that makes you want to fall asleep). Set up the best study environment possible: good lighting and a comfortable work area. If background music helps you focus, you may want to turn it on, but otherwise keep the room quiet. If you are using a computer to take notes, be sure you don't have any other windows open, especially applications like social media, games, or anything else that could distract you. Silence your phone and turn off notifications. Be sure to keep water close by so you stay hydrated while you study (but avoid unhealthy drinks and snacks).

Also, take into account the best time of day to study. Are you freshest first thing in the morning? Try to set aside some time then to work through the material. Is your mind clearer in the afternoon or evening? Schedule your study session then. Another method is to study at the same time of day that you will take the test, so that your brain gets used to working on the material at that time and will be ready to focus at test time.

STEP 5: STUDY!

Once you have done all the study preparation, it's time to settle into the actual studying. Sit down, take a few moments to settle your mind so you can focus, and begin to follow your study plan. Don't give in to distractions or let yourself procrastinate. This is your time to prepare so you'll be ready to fearlessly approach the test. Make the most of the time and stay focused.

Of course, you don't want to burn out. If you study too long you may find that you're not retaining the information very well. Take regular study breaks. For example, taking five minutes out of every hour to walk briskly, breathing deeply and swinging your arms, can help your mind stay fresh.

As you get to the end of each chapter or section, it's a good idea to do a quick review. Remind yourself of what you learned and work on any difficult parts. When you feel that you've mastered the material, move on to the next part. At the end of your study session, briefly skim through your notes again.

But while review is helpful, cramming last minute is NOT. If at all possible, work ahead so that you won't need to fit all your study into the last day. Cramming overloads your brain with more information than it can process and retain, and your tired mind may struggle to recall even previously learned information when it is overwhelmed with last-minute study. Also, the urgent nature of cramming and the stress placed on your brain contribute to anxiety. You'll be more likely to go to the test feeling unprepared and having trouble thinking clearly.

So don't cram, and don't stay up late before the test, even just to review your notes at a leisurely pace. Your brain needs rest more than it needs to go over the information again. In fact, plan to finish your studies by noon or early afternoon the day before the test. Give your brain the rest of the day to relax or focus on other things, and get a good night's sleep. Then you will be fresh for the test and better able to recall what you've studied.

STEP 6: TAKE A PRACTICE TEST

Many courses offer sample tests, either online or in the study materials. This is an excellent resource to check whether you have mastered the material, as well as to prepare for the test format and environment.

Check the test format ahead of time: the number of questions, the type (multiple choice, free response, etc.), and the time limit. Then create a plan for working through them. For example, if you have 30 minutes to take a 60-question test, your limit is 30 seconds per question. Spend less time on the questions you know well so that you can take more time on the difficult ones.

If you have time to take several practice tests, take the first one open book, with no time limit. Work through the questions at your own pace and make sure you fully understand them. Gradually work up to taking a test under test conditions: sit at a desk with all study materials put away and set a timer. Pace yourself to make sure you finish the test with time to spare and go back to check your answers if you have time.

After each test, check your answers. On the questions you missed, be sure you understand why you missed them. Did you misread the question (tests can use tricky wording)? Did you forget the information? Or was it something you hadn't learned? Go back and study any shaky areas that the practice tests reveal.

Taking these tests not only helps with your grade, but also aids in combating test anxiety. If you're already used to the test conditions, you're less likely to worry about it, and working through tests until you're scoring well gives you a confidence boost. Go through the practice tests until you feel comfortable, and then you can go into the test knowing that you're ready for it.

Test Tips

On test day, you should be confident, knowing that you've prepared well and are ready to answer the questions. But aside from preparation, there are several test day strategies you can employ to maximize your performance.

First, as stated before, get a good night's sleep the night before the test (and for several nights before that, if possible). Go into the test with a fresh, alert mind rather than staying up late to study.

Try not to change too much about your normal routine on the day of the test. It's important to eat a nutritious breakfast, but if you normally don't eat breakfast at all, consider eating just a protein bar. If you're a coffee drinker, go ahead and have your normal coffee. Just make sure you time it so that the caffeine doesn't wear off right in the middle of your test. Avoid sugary beverages, and drink enough water to stay hydrated but not so much that you need a restroom break 10 minutes into the test. If your test isn't first thing in the morning, consider going for a walk or doing a light workout before the test to get your blood flowing.

Allow yourself enough time to get ready, and leave for the test with plenty of time to spare so you won't have the anxiety of scrambling to arrive in time. Another reason to be early is to select a good seat. It's helpful to sit away from doors and windows, which can be distracting. Find a good seat, get out your supplies, and settle your mind before the test begins.

When the test begins, start by going over the instructions carefully, even if you already know what to expect. Make sure you avoid any careless mistakes by following the directions.

Then begin working through the questions, pacing yourself as you've practiced. If you're not sure on an answer, don't spend too much time on it, and don't let it shake your confidence. Either skip it and come back later, or eliminate as many wrong answers as possible and guess among the remaining ones. Don't dwell on these questions as you continue—put them out of your mind and focus on what lies ahead.

Be sure to read all of the answer choices, even if you're sure the first one is the right answer. Sometimes you'll find a better one if you keep reading. But don't second-guess yourself if you do immediately know the answer. Your gut instinct is usually right. Don't let test anxiety rob you of the information you know.

If you have time at the end of the test (and if the test format allows), go back and review your answers. Be cautious about changing any, since your first instinct tends to be correct, but make sure you didn't misread any of the questions or accidentally mark the wrong answer choice. Look over any you skipped and make an educated guess.

At the end, leave the test feeling confident. You've done your best, so don't waste time worrying about your performance or wishing you could change anything. Instead, celebrate the successful completion of this test. And finally, use this test to learn how to deal with anxiety even better next time.

Review Video: 5 Tips to Beat Test Anxiety
Visit mometrix.com/academy and enter code: 570656

Important Qualification

Not all anxiety is created equal. If your test anxiety is causing major issues in your life beyond the classroom or testing center, or if you are experiencing troubling physical symptoms related to your anxiety, it may be a sign of a serious physiological or psychological condition. If this sounds like your situation, we strongly encourage you to seek professional help.

Thank You

We at Mometrix would like to extend our heartfelt thanks to you, our friend and patron, for allowing us to play a part in your journey. It is a privilege to serve people from all walks of life who are unified in their commitment to building the best future they can for themselves.

The preparation you devote to these important testing milestones may be the most valuable educational opportunity you have for making a real difference in your life. We encourage you to put your heart into it—that feeling of succeeding, overcoming, and yes, conquering will be well worth the hours you've invested.

We want to hear your story, your struggles and your successes, and if you see any opportunities for us to improve our materials so we can help others even more effectively in the future, please share that with us as well. **The team at Mometrix would be absolutely thrilled to hear from you!** So please, send us an email (support@mometrix.com) and let's stay in touch.

> **If you'd like some additional help, check out these other resources we offer for your exam:**
>
> http://MometrixFlashcards.com/CertifiedArborist

Additional Bonus Material

Due to our efforts to try to keep this book to a manageable length, we've created a link that will give you access to all of your additional bonus material.

Please visit http://www.mometrix.com/bonus948/certarborist to access the information.